inspiring harmony

A Memoir about Leading with Grace

by
Michael Melton

Casa Luna Press
Tucson, Arizona

Copyright ©2019 Michael Melton

All Rights Reserved.

No part of this publication may be reproduced or transmitted in any form or by any means, electronic or mechanical, including photocopying, recording, taping, or any information storage or retrieval system without the permission of the author except in the case of brief quotations embodied in critical articles and reviews.

This book is typeset in Minion Pro and Goldenbook.

Design and production by Wynne Brown LLC and printed by IngramSpark.

Casa Luna Press
1619 North Catalina Avenue
Tucson, Arizona 85712
USA

ISBN: 978-0-9847067-1-6 (softcover)

Dedication

To the many teachers in my life who have shown me how to inspire harmony, and to my friends and family, especially my wife, Arlis, and my parents, Merle and Martha, who have shown me grace through their love and support.

The cover photo, taken by my wife, Arlis McLean, is of a cairn, while we were walking the Camino de Santiago (the Way of St. James) along the west coast of Spain, just north of the border with Portugal. The term "cairn," originally from the Scottish Gaelic word "carn," means "heap of stones."

Cairns (sometimes called "balancing rocks" or "stacking stones") have been used for a variety of purposes since prehistoric times. One continuous use from ancient times to the present is to mark a path for travelers. The image seemed fitting for this book because my intention is to help guide you along your journey toward inspiring harmony and leading with grace.

My wish for you is that you will always be on the lookout for the markers in your life that will guide you toward grace.

And as the pilgrims to Santiago say to one another, Buen Camino.

Contents

Preface

Art and Life Require Discipline	3
If You're Good, People Will Notice	7
It's Rarely Black or White	11
Live in the Moment	15
It Isn't About the Money	20
Your Image Will Take Care of Itself	25
Life Isn't Fair	30
You're Never Too Old	34
Choose Your Battles Wisely	37
There's More Than One Way	41
Walk a Mile in My Shoes	45
Leaders Must Have Thick Skin	49

Admit Your Mistakes	53
Never Settle for Mezzo Beige	59
Making Music Is Healing	64
Life Is About Tension and Release	68
Be A Servant	72
Who Gets the Credit? Or the Blame?	76
First, Land the Airplane	79
Failure Is Absolutely an Option	83
Coping with Tragedy	88
To Worry or Not to Worry	92
The Whole Truth?	96
You Cannot Be Anything You Want to Be	100
It Isn't About Perfection	103
Be Part of a Community	106
Make My Day	111
Be a Teacher	114

Suck It Up	119
You Never Arrive	125
Bloom Where You're Planted	129
Live in Grace	133
Acknowledgments	137
Photo Credits	138

Preface

I love harmony.

The musical confluence of voices or instruments creating rich and varied textures, dissonance and consonance, is a beautiful metaphor for life. Harmony can be open and stark or close and sweet, but the musicians are always part of the ensemble. There is nothing quite like harmony to inspire our souls.

I've spent most of my life teaching and performing music, at first because I enjoyed being in front of an audience, and later because of my love for music. This book is a compilation of what I hope are interesting and entertaining stories from my own life, along with the lessons those stories have taught me about leading. In some cases I did the right thing—and in some cases not. In most of my experiences, it was simply a matter of learning how to live better, how to make the most of my relationships with others—especially when leading groups of people—and how to be content, whatever the circumstances.

Many of us will, at some point, find ourselves leading a group, whether it be a committee, a class, or perhaps a musical ensemble. In most tasks we undertake, there is an element of leadership if we perform those tasks effectively. My stories are meant to remind you of what's important when leading others. Some of the lessons are more about finding peace within ourselves, which I believe is a prerequisite to being an effective leader.

At the end of each chapter are questions and comments to provoke further thought, encourage more self-exploration, or facilitate team building.

The last chapter is titled "Live in Grace," and that perfectly summarizes what I most want to say: Living in grace means to be spiritually and emotionally healthy, to be truly happy from the inside out, to foster good relationships with others, and to contribute to the well being of our communities. I can think of no better prescription for being a leader.

I hope you will continually strive to live in grace and to inspire harmony in the groups you lead.

Michael Melton

June 2019

Michael Melton

Ⓗ Art and Life Require Discipline

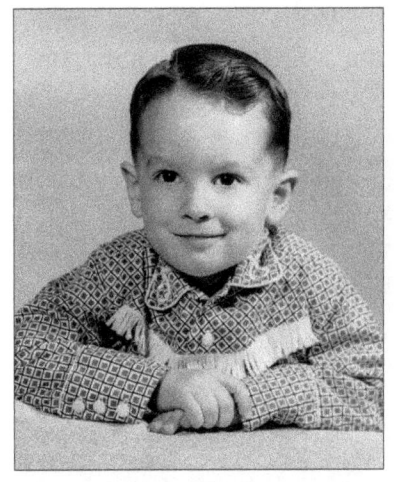

Mike at age four

My roots are in small-town middle America. I grew up as a preacher's kid with traditional Midwestern Christian values and the narrow view of the world that so often accompanied that way of life, especially sixty years ago. My worldview was limited to what I had been exposed to: my school, my church, my friends, hunting and fishing, gospel and country music.[1] Back in those days, small towns were supportive communities; they were the sort of places where police put on their flashing lights and got out of their squad car and saluted and where all other drivers pulled off the road out of respect for a passing funeral procession.

I was a precocious child, a quick learner, and confident in most situations.

I also became a good musician at an early age with a strong desire to practice and learn, but an even stronger desire to perform. I enjoyed singing and playing piano for school and church functions, and I relished the strokes I got for performing. I've always relied too much on the approval of others for validation, and, as a young person, performing music was a great way to garner that validation. So, I was happy for every opportunity to sing or play.

But because music came easily for me, it eventually became

[1] *I grew up on what I call "white gospel music," a style that's very similar to traditional country music.*

Inspiring Harmony

> [2] Sight-reading is the term commonly used to mean playing or singing a piece of music at first sight.

> [3] A piece for an instrumental soloist (in this case, piano) consisting of multiple movements. "Sonata" literally means a piece to be played, as opposed to "Cantata," a piece to be sung.

evident I could get along just fine without having to work so hard. I was a good sight-reader[2] and could always "fake it" if I needed to.

The first time I was seriously admonished for that was when I was in high school and a private student of Dr. Robert Mueller, a piano professor at Southern Illinois University (SIU) in Carbondale. He had assigned me a Mozart piano sonata[3], and I was cavalier enough to ignore it for a week and then sight-read it at my next lesson.

I played the first movement reasonably well and, when I finished, looked at him with a certain self-satisfaction.

"How was that?" I asked.

"Not bad, Mike," he answered. "Now just imagine how good you could be if you practiced."

I did work a little harder when I became a student at SIU, but it wasn't until I transferred to the University of Iowa and began studying with James Avery that I learned the sort of disciplined practice that's required to really improve. Mr. Avery expected a higher level of performance, and I suppose I was old enough by then to understand it was time to get to work. So I did.

To be disciplined in the study of music is a necessary rigor. To think that merely "feeling it" is sufficient is naïve. Many music students make the mistake of thinking that performing with emotion is the most important thing. On the contrary, the most critical element of music-making is learning and practicing the fundamentals of music and technique. Without such a solid foundation on which to hang expression, emotional performances become merely sentimental and trite.

The true joy of an expressive musical performance springs from countless hours of disciplined study and practice.

Robert Mueller

Michael Melton

Being a disciplined leader also requires mindful exercise. "Shooting from the hip," as some undisciplined leaders tend to do, can create a quagmire of problems.

One particularly elusive mental discipline for many leaders is learning to recognize "the art of the con." I realize that sounds insidious, but I mean it in a more light-hearted way. Cons can be intentional or not, harmful or innocuous, and they often creep into the proceedings unnoticed. Leaders must be vigilant concerning the motives of people both within and outside their team.

I remember observing many adults when I was young and imagining no one would be able to put one over on them. They seemed too savvy, too street smart; they had too much common sense. For them, the old adage, "If it seems too good to be true, it probably is," was a principle to live by.

In the mid-1980s, I did a little bit of jingle singing[4] for television commercials and industrial film, which required me to have a "jingle demo." I had conducted a new composition for a jingle producer/composer in Chicago, who then offered to help me make my first demo; he would provide some instrumental tracks for me to sing over and charge me "only" $1,000 to record my singing. (In all honesty, I wasn't conned—I did agree to the arrangement, but the story makes my point, nonetheless.) I was happy with my recording and took it with me on a trip to Iowa, where I always had my beige 1976 Volkswagen Beetle repaired. (I once drove it

> [4] *Jingle singing isn't as common as it once was, having been largely replaced on television ads by existing musical recordings. In their heyday, they were catchy tunes meant to stick with the consumer: "I am stuck on BAND-AIDs®…;" "Two scoops of raisins;" "Plop, plop, fizz, fizz…" Singers in demand made a lot of money from the residuals paid on those commercials.*
> *I was not one of those singers…*

James Avery

there all the way from Chicago without brakes—just to have them replaced at that garage.) This VW mechanic lived in the country and didn't appear to be terribly impressed by shiny objects. Anyway, I told him my story and played the recording for him.

"Pretty good," he said.

"Yes," I replied proudly. "The producer who helped me make it said I would make a lot of money in the jingle business."

"Is that the same guy who took your thousand dollars?" he asked wryly.

I did at least make enough money to pay for my demo ...

I've learned there is value in exercising discipline—to be circumspect in one's dealings—to be completely devoted to one's work. The easy, indulgent path is to take whatever you can wherever you can get it, to earn a quick buck without taking the longer view of your career, to be a splashy musician without the hard work that practice entails. But there is virtue and great satisfaction in taking a more disciplined approach to art, to life, and to leadership. Discipline is one of the foundational principles of leading with grace.

Food for thought

- How do you set goals for yourself? For your team?
- When did you last change a goal based on new circumstances or information?
- Have you created opportunities for your group to define its purpose and mission? To create a disciplined plan of action?

Michael Melton

(h) If You're Good, People Will Notice

I truly enjoyed music-making early on, but, as I noted in the first chapter, I also enjoyed being noticed and praised for it. My first "performance" was at age seven at the First Christian Church of McLeansboro, Illinois. The church organist, Mrs. Malone, had been giving me piano lessons for several months and wanted to create an opportunity for me to perform, so she arranged a simple tune that would be comprised of only tonic and dominant-seventh chords.[1] Then she taught me how to play an "oom-pah-pah" accompaniment while she filled in the melody and everything else—a sort of "piano four hands" suitable for church. I had no music to read, so she got us started and, at the appropriate moments, would lean over and whisper "Change" when it was time to move from tonic to dominant and back.

Eula Malone

When we finished our piece, the congregation applauded, and I remember thinking, *I really like this!*

Many years later, when I was a college music major, I went back to the church in McLeansboro and was asked to play something for the service. Eager to be impressive, especially to Mrs. Malone, I improvised on a hymn tune as bombastically as I was

> [1] *The most basic of harmonic elements in music. Many Classical symphonies end by alternating the tonic and dominant-seventh chords to give the piece a strong sense of finality.*

Inspiring Harmony

able, throwing in flourishes, a thundering bass, and other feats of technical bravado.

After the service, I couldn't wait to hear just how wonderful she thought I was. Her comment to me was, "Now Michael, just remember, there's a time for playing loudly and a time for playing softly."

I was somewhat deflated, even though I could tell she was proud of how far I had come. It was one of the first times I began to realize that people will notice if you're good. It really isn't necessary or even wise to try too hard to prove it.

That lesson was hammered home a bit less delicately around the same time at Southern Illinois University in Carbondale. Hubert Humphrey was the keynote speaker for a fundraising dinner at the university, and the Men's Glee Club, in which I sang, had been asked to perform.

As the dinner was about to begin, the stage manager came to our conductor, Robert Kingsbury, and said they were ready for the national anthem.

"All right," he said. "We'll wait here until you're ready for us."

"No," she responded. "We were expecting you to lead the anthem."

With no recorded accompaniment available and little chance of a successful a cappella performance, he turned to our accompanist who immediately said there was no way she could play it without music.

So he looked at me and asked in his Mississippi drawl, "Michael, son, do you think you could play our national anthem?"

"What key would you like it in?" I offered in my cockiest tone.

"Just play it in B-flat like everybody else, and don't be a smartass," he shot back.

Hubert Humphrey

Robert Kingsbury

I got the message for sure and played it in B-flat.[2]

Mr. K's microphone was still on after the anthem ended and picked up his voice when, during the invocation, he turned to me and said, "Damn good job, Michael, son."

I tutored and tested graduate students in the Music Department at the University of Chicago for six years in the 1980s.[3] If students weren't already neurotic when they arrived there, most were by the time they left. The pressure to prove one's intellectual superiority was intense. And the competition wasn't as much among the students as among the professors: which faculty members were published in the most respected journals, which ones were in demand as lecturers, and which traveled in the most elite circles around the world.

The department chair for a few of the years I was there was Howard Brown, a preeminent musicologist specializing in music of the Renaissance. The most

[2] *The melody of "The Star-Spangled Banner" has a wide range and is therefore often transposed for solo singers. But the usual key for group singing is B-flat.*

[3] *I prepared graduate students in what were termed "Practicum Skills": sight-singing, piano sight-reading, music dictation, playing figured bass, playing from "C" clefs at the piano, and orchestral score reading.*

Howard Mayer Brown - Portrait by Jacqueline Morreau

notable characteristic about Howard to me was his accessibility and unassuming manner. He certainly had his quirks and eccentricities, but he was self-effacing and not at all pretentious. He spoke many languages and often traveled to European countries and lectured about Renaissance music in the language of whatever country he was visiting. Despite the fact that he was light years ahead of me academically and in terms of his position at the university and in the musical world, I always felt I could walk into his office, pull up a chair, and have an easy conversation with him.

Howard passed away many years ago in a rather poetic fashion, I'm told. He was visiting Venice during *Carnevale* and stopped into a shop to buy a mask. When he came out, he collapsed on the sidewalk from a heart attack. As people gathered around him, he was still conscious and speaking to them in their own languages. Emergency workers put him into a gondola to connect to a faster boat on the Grand Canal that would then transport him to a hospital. But this Renaissance man died on the gondola, looking at the city of Venice.

What I remember most about him, though, is he never felt the need to prove himself better than someone else. He simply loved what he did and was very good at it, and others did indeed notice.

It is so unfortunate that we define ourselves more by what we do than by who we are. And it is so misguided to measure our worth primarily by the opinions of others, rather than simply being authentic with ourselves.

What I learned from Howard's example: Many who desire positions of leadership do so to be the center of attention. For those who seek the limelight, the best advice may be to let the limelight find you. If you're good, those you lead will notice.

Food for thought:

- If I asked you to tell me about yourself, what would you say?
- How much do you rely on the attention and praise of others to validate your work?
- If you were unable to continue as the leader of your group, could someone else pick up where you left off?

Michael Melton

It's Rarely Black or White

Every summer, from about the ages of seven to seventeen, I attended Southern Illinois Christian Service Camp in West Frankfurt, Illinois.[1] It was an intense week or two of Bible study, evangelistic-style services, sharing common meals with other kids in the cafeteria, sleeping in bunk beds, and enjoying some summer recreation. Some of the ministers from local churches who were our leaders for the camp were conservative and dogmatic, which often led to interesting, if not fiery, discussions.

I always listened intently and made every effort to come down on the right side of the debate, lest I risk the eternal damnation of my soul.

One summer when I was in high school, the topic du jour

> [1] *I was a preacher's kid, raised in a non-denominational Christian church. Summer camp was very popular among youth from Christian churches in Southern Illinois...*

11

Inspiring Harmony

Mike's high school portrait

was situational ethics. The discussion, held among all the campers, centered on appropriate behavior in a dating relationship. I found it fascinating (and not a little bit titillating) to hear the discussion leaders attempting to make a distinction among "kissing only," "light petting," "heavy petting," and "sex."

As you might imagine, there was a rather lively debate among some of the high school students, but I sat silent since this was all new territory for me (except in my mind, of course).

As a few of the campers found the courage to say they thought a little "fooling around" wasn't necessarily a bad thing, one of the ministers, Floyd Stabler, stood up and said, "Here's what the Bible has to say about it."

And he proceeded to read a Scripture passage that addressed the subject only tangentially, but seemed to close the lid on the matter.

The issue, at least for Floyd, was clearly black or white.

Some of the campers applauded, while others looked deflated, but the discussion abruptly ended.

In the immaturity of one's youth, it's easy to be zealous about right and wrong, whether with regard to religion, politics, or social issues. But with maturity comes the increasing realization that what once appeared absolutely black or white is really mostly gray. There are varying shades of gray, in fact, and very few things are axiomatic. The failure to mature individually or as a society has not only led to "fundamental" disagreements, but even to war, often in the name of God. In a group setting, the arrogance of "my way or the highway" thinking is already a non-starter when a difference of opinion exists, but to play the "God" card—*I'm right because God is on my side*—introduces an often insurmountable obstacle to compromise or reconciliation.

I grew up around that kind of thinking, and I've since come to believe that fundamentalism, in any form, is evil. Even if it doesn't start a war, it can still wreak havoc with people's lives. And for a leader, it can lead to an untenable situation.

A conundrum related to the matter of black or white is what to do when a question has no good answer.

Michael Melton

I was teaching music at the junior high school in Ankeny, Iowa, fresh out of college at age twenty-two. The day after a choral concert, my ninth-grade chorus had a study period during our regular class time so they could prepare for final exams. One of my female students, who was about fourteen going on twenty-one, was looking particularly glum and seemed to want me to notice. She was wearing a shirt tied up above her midriff and unbuttoned down to the knot.[2]

[2] *The style was popularized by the likes of Daisy Duke from the television show "The Dukes of Hazzard." It didn't take much to push the limits of what was considered acceptable school attire.*

As I walked through the classroom, I asked if she was OK.

She answered in a pouty voice, "The vice principal told me I have to go home and change because my clothes are just too revealing, but I don't think they are. What do you think?"

Well, I wasn't about to weigh in on that one, so my answer was, "If the vice principal thinks you should go home and change, I guess that's what you'll have to do."

I could tell it wasn't the answer or kind of attention she was hoping for, but I did feel I had managed to come up with the best answer I could, even if I hedged the question.

Catherine Bach as Daisy Duke

Nurturing harmony can be messy: The more decisions I face, especially when leading a group of people with varying opinions, the more I'm aware the choices I make are rarely completely the right ones, or the alternatives the wrong ones. It's more often a matter of making the best choice under the circumstances, which could be a different choice under different circumstances.

In other words, it's rarely black or white. It may take us out of our comfort zone, and it may not be as neat and tidy as we leaders would like, but the truth is, life is mostly gray.

Inspiring Harmony

Food for thought:

- Can you remember a time when you made an important decision you might now handle differently, knowing things aren't so black and white?

- Are you seeing more gray in your decision-making than in the past? Can you get comfortable with the idea that, more often than "yes" or "no," the answer may be "it depends"?

- If members of your group would like to move in a different direction than you are taking them, are you open to compromise?

Michael Melton

♭ Live in the Moment

I started playing piano for revival services in Southern Illinois when I was thirteen years old. Revivals were usually a week of nightly services held by a church to "revive" the spirit of the congregation.

I was happy to volunteer at first, but eventually I charged $10 per night to show up and play. I also had a men's vocal quartet made up of high school students. Men's quartets were very popular then among evangelical churches, and I loved arranging and performing gospel music for the group.[1] I would sometimes sing, sometimes play, sometimes both.

One night, when I was a sixteen-year-old junior in high school, my quartet was invited to sing at a small church in the country for a revival service. We used to refer to this kind of church as "charismatic," which meant the congregation was quite vocal and emotional with frequent dancing, speaking in tongues,[2] healing, and swooning. I was expecting quite a show, but by the end of the service, everything had remained quite calm and orderly.

When the preacher rose to give the benediction,

> [1] *"Gospel music" is defined differently by different people. One need only preface the term with "black," "white," "traditional," "contemporary," "urban," "southern," "country," etc., to change its meaning. I grew up with an amalgam of several of these brands of gospel.*

> [2] *"Speaking in tongues" is the commonly used phrase for "Glossolalia." The practice is said to be Biblically based and a manifestation of (the baptism of) the holy spirit. It is supposedly a language unkown to the speaker and, some say, a language known only to God.*

Inspiring Harmony

he said he thought the spirit had "not yet come into this place," and he suggested we should sing a little more. He invited another singer from the congregation to come forward and lead us all in a song I'll never forget, "The City of Gold." [3]

Country church

The man invited to lead looked like he had parked his tractor outside before coming in. He wore overalls and was as big as the side of a barn—not overweight, but very muscular and about 6 ½ feet tall with broad shoulders.

> [3] "The City of Gold" is a traditional gospel song that has been recorded many times. With the right stylistic embellishments, this straightforward-looking, four-part hymn can become quite the rousing number.

As he walked down the only aisle in the church, he grabbed my arm, lifting my entire body off the pew with one hand, and said, "Come on, boy, you play."

So, of course, I did.

Well, we sang all four verses of "The City of Gold," and the congregation was beginning to respond. Several people were standing (a few actually on the pews), arms were swaying in the air, and some were shouting things I couldn't understand.

After four verses and refrains, the leader roared, "Let's sing that chorus again!"

So we sang it over and over, probably six or eight more times.

The place was rocking by then, and, I must say, I was having some fun at the piano. In all the excitement, I hadn't noticed that a woman had come up from the congregation and was standing directly behind me watching me play.

Suddenly, the spirit came and got her, and she let out a long, shrill shriek like I had never heard before right behind my head. I was so startled, I stopped playing and half stood up.

The song leader spun around, pointed at me, and growled, "Sit down, boy, keep playing!"

He's bigger than God, I thought, *so I'd better just keep playing.*

(What I didn't learn until later was the three boys with me couldn't stop laughing at what they were seeing.) After a couple more choruses, the song leader and the preacher seemed satisfied that the spirit had indeed come into that place, and the benediction was finally given.

Michael Melton

Inspiring Harmony

What I remember most about that night was being completely caught up in the moment. It was a little frightening, but it was mostly exhilarating and exciting. My tendency has always been to worry about things before they happen and often to lament not having handled things as well as I could have after the fact. But it seems to me the better way to approach life is to only be concerned about the present because that's all there is. The past and the future really don't exist, only the present. Worrying about what is coming or what is past is a futile waste of energy and can even be debilitating.

"Uncle Joe" Ellis

My wife had an older, distant cousin whom everyone knew as "Uncle Joe." What a gentleman—and what a gentle man he was. When we went out for a meal, I'd ask Joe what he was having to drink.

His inevitable answer was, "Well, Mike, what are you having?"

If I said I'd be having a glass of wine, he'd say, "Well, I think I'll have one, too." He'd never have a drink unless someone else was joining him.

Joe and I always played piano duets together when he came to our house for a visit. He had played the organ for silent movies, so he could play many of the old standards.

"What shall we play?" I'd ask.

"Anything you like," he'd answer.

Once we had chosen a song, I'd ask, "What key tonight, Joe?"

"Any key you like," he'd say, and off we'd go—no forethought, no preparation, just being in the moment.

I remember taking Joe to see *A Christmas Carol* at the Goodman Theater [4] in Chicago one year when he was well past ninety. At the intermission I asked him how he was enjoying the show.

His answer was perfect: "Well, Mike, I can't see anything, and I can't hear anything, but I'm having a great time!"

> [4] Goodman Theater's heart-warming production of *A Christmas Carol* has been an annual tradition in Chicago since 1978. In 1982, I was privileged to take a group of singers from the Chicago Children's Choir to sing Christmas carols before and after the show and at intermission. It's a wonderful memory.

Our society makes it difficult to live in the moment. So much hand-wringing about things to come and regrets about what might have been. How much time and energy are wasted by committees and organizations spinning their wheels rehashing the same agendas time and again. Another important step toward living and leading with grace is to remember: We have less control than we think over the future and no control over the past, so we may as well enjoy the present—it's really all we have.

Food for thought:

- Are you mindful and truly present in the daily events of your life? If not, what conscious choices could you make to be more present?

- Does your organization spend too much time re-litigating old business?

- Do you encourage your group to "leave it all on the field"? To make the most of whatever they are doing, in the moment?

Inspiring Harmony

ⓗ It Isn't About the Money

I've never made much money, but I've had a wonderful life doing what I love to do.

I've always been very fortunate to have work available when I've needed it, and I've been happy to try my hand at many different things. I suppose I could have been better at doing any one thing, had I chosen to pursue it exclusively, but I doubt I would have been as fulfilled in my life. That may not be true for everyone, but I believe one thing is true for all of us: If your primary reason for choosing a career path is to make money, you might want to rethink your priorities.

Mike's "On Camera" headshot

My very first job was cutting grass in the summertime for several people in the town of Carterville, Illinois, where I grew up—I was thirteen years old at the time. Since then, my list of jobs includes: grocery-store stocker, grocery-store delivery boy (different store), radio station announcer (more of a Sunday afternoon station monitor really), church musician (that went on for twenty-five years), greenhouse assistant for a florist, road construction crew, house painter, corn de-tasseler, furniture store bookkeeper and delivery man, service station attendant and tow truck driver, jingle singer, voiceover and on-camera actor, flight instructor, junior high and later college teacher, and, as a musician: singer, pianist, conductor, and score reader.[1]

I've been told by many people that, if I would just choose one path and devote myself solely to it, I would be much more successful in my career.

I suppose that depends on how one measures success.

It's true I might have performed better at the one thing I chose to perfect, and I'm sure I would have made more money in the long run. But I would have missed out on the rich diversity of experiences I've enjoyed. How wonderful to have been able to teach a student how to fly an airplane one day and conduct an opera the next.

And where music is concerned, while devoting myself to one instrument or area of study might have improved my skill in that particular area, I think teaching and performing in a variety of styles and on different instruments have made me a well-rounded and empathetic musician.[2]

I sang for years with a good friend, Ed Pounds, in the Grant Park Symphony Chorus (Chicago) and many other places. He and I sang in a men's quartet together, and he was the bass soloist in one of my church choirs. He was a large African-American man with a large, deep bass voice.

[1] I humbly submit I may now add "author" to the list.

[2] The language of music is universal regardless of the musical "dialect" being spoken. When musicians lose the all-too-prevalent snobbery, we find much in common among many styles of music, especially with regard to expression (e.g., the art of shaping a phrase).

Ed Pounds

Inspiring Harmony

Ed invited me to play the piano for the funeral services of both his parents. The funeral home where the services were held was on the south side of Chicago, and I'm pretty sure mine was the only white face in the place. But I had grown up playing church music, much of it in gospel style, so I felt right at home. It was gratifying, and actually fun, to begin playing "Precious Lord, Take My Hand"[3] and hear the congregation voicing their approval with "uh-huh" and "amen."

As I was leaving the funeral home after Ed's mother's service, I felt someone behind me grab my hand. I turned to see an elderly black man who had attended the service looking up at me—he must have been pushing ninety and stood not much more than five feet tall.

Before I could say a word, he smiled and said, "I coulda swore these hands was black."

I shook his hand and thanked him. His hand was withered, but strong, and his face etched with decades of living a life I could only imagine. It was the nicest compliment I could have hoped for.

I doubt I was paid for playing those services, but that really didn't matter.

Tragically, Ed died at an early age in Chicago during the heat wave of 1995.

The primary criterion for choosing how to spend your life should be to first discover where your passion lies. Then ask if the thing that gets you up in the morning is realistically achievable. As I'll discuss later, having the desire to do something doesn't necessarily mean it's possible. But if you are successful in pursuing your passion, look for opportunities to lead, to share it with others.

[3] Also known as "Take My Hand, Precious Lord," this iconic gospel song was written by the Rev. Thomas A. Dorsey, based on the hymn tune "Maitland" from 1844. He wrote it in Chicago shortly after his wife, Nettie, died during childbirth—his newborn son died that same night. It was the favorite song of Martin Luther King, Jr. and was sung by Mahalia Jackson at his funeral. It has been recorded by many artists and is still frequently played and sung, particularly at funerals.

Inspiring Harmony

Here is the lesson I've learned: It isn't about the money. Please don't misunderstand, I don't believe there's anything wrong with making a lot of money or being wealthy, but it shouldn't be your reason for living, and it shouldn't be your primary reason for choosing a career path. Find your passion, consider your potential strengths, and work toward a life that's fulfilling, satisfying, and complete.

In the end, we're all going to die anyway, so who cares if you die with a lot of money?

Food for thought:

- When you look back on your life thus far, what are you most proud of?

- Of the top five goals you hope to achieve in life, where does money rank?

- Does your organization's mission include making the world a better place?

Michael Melton

(h) Your Image Will Take Care of Itself

I know, what an odd thing to say ...

We're all concerned about our images, at least to some extent. But when appearance becomes more important than substance, we have a problem. A leader can quickly become ineffectual when a group perceives he or she is flamboyant, but shallow.

When I was an undergrad at the University of Iowa in the late 1970s, I was very driven to become a renowned conductor and tried just about everything to look and act the part. I liked the idea of being "the maestro" almost as much as I enjoyed music-making itself.

The Director of Choral Activities at the time was Don V Moses. Dr. Moses was a popular and successful choral conductor, and I very much wanted to emulate him. (We actually share the same birthday exactly twenty years apart.) In fact, when I showed up at the university one day wearing a black shirt, something he often did, a few of the other students began referring to me as "little Don V."

Don V Moses

A few years later, after teaching junior high school, I returned to the University of Iowa to pursue a master's degree in Choral Conducting.

After my degree recital, during my debrief with Dr. Moses, he said he thought he had made a mistake by not spending more time with me preparing for the recital—that he had given me too much

Inspiring Harmony

> [1] I have watched countless conductors work, many of them world famous, and I am always amazed at the radically different gestural techniques they employ. Invariably, the best ones have found a way, however unorthodox it may be, to inspire their ensembles to make beautiful music.

> [2] *Franz Schubert was a late Classical, early Romantic composer whose melodies and phrase structure often demand a delicate sensitivity. The "Dies irae," from Giuseppe Verdi's* Messa da Requiem, *is an explosive depiction of the "day of wrath." A conductor's gestures for the two pieces would be starkly different.*

credit for being able to handle it on my own.

"Didn't I look good?" I asked. "My gestures were clear, precise, professional—"

"It isn't a matter of looking good," he answered. "What matters is the sound you elicit from the choir."

It's true, I did have conducting technique fairly well in hand, but my ability to listen critically and rehearse effectively were still lacking.[1]

I spent the next several years in the Chicago Symphony Chorus singing with numerous world-famous conductors, including the CSO's music director, Sir Georg Solti. I observed how each conductor carried himself in rehearsal and performance, on and off the stage. I found myself imitating them, usually subconsciously, and most often on the podium. I remember auditioning for the orchestral conducting program at the Aspen Music Festival during that time and conducting poorly, in part because I had adopted so much of Solti's style that I conducted a simple Schubert Octet as if it were the "Dies irae" from the Verdi *Requiem*.[2] Solti was a wonderful musician, but his conducting technique was hardly textbook: He often looked like a madman out of control.

Again, I was so preoccupied

Sir Georg Solti

with portraying the *image* of a conductor that I failed to recognize the more important matter of recreating the substance and style of Schubert's music. I was not accepted into the orchestral conducting program that year, but I think I'd have had a better chance had I brought my own musical sensibility and conducting technique to the audition, rather than trying to recreate someone else's.[3]

Several years later I began to be hired frequently to provide musicians and play piano for fundraising events in the Chicago area, often on behalf of the Republican Party.[4] I learned a lot during those events simply by watching the politicians as they gave their speeches, and more so as they interacted with guests at the dinner. It was interesting to see people like George H.W. Bush, Robert Dole,[5] and, later, Hillary Clinton (who was not at a Republican fundraiser, obviously) as they worked the crowd.

It was so clear when the featured person was sincerely interested in the issues impacting their constituents and when they were more interested in projecting a particular image. I often couldn't tell if the guests were as aware of the "glad handing" going on and were simply playing their parts, or if they were so enthralled by the celebrity that they were swept up in the moment.

Regardless, it made me think again about the importance of being true and authentic, of caring more about substance than appearance.

It also highlighted for me, yet again, how similar politicians are to evangelists.

I have come to learn over the years, after many misguided attempts at being "the maestro," that

> [3] I did spend three wonderful summers at the Aspen Music Festival in the 1980s as a singer and conducting student with the Choral Institute, under the direction of Fiora Contino—a lovely person and excellent teacher.

Fiora Contino

> [4] I don't usually vote Republican, but I was happy to have the work.

> [5] Robert Dole was one of the kindest people I met while playing these fundraising dinners. He actually took a minute to get acquainted with the pianist.

Inspiring Harmony

your image will take care of itself. By virtue of your personality, life experience, and professional skills, an image develops that is largely beyond your control, unless your image, in fact, becomes your primary focus.

The other realization that, ideally, comes sooner rather than later is that most people are more astute than some of us may think.

It really isn't that hard to see through a person who is more style than substance, and it doesn't take long for that person to be dismissed as trite or insubstantial.

Mike with George H. W. Bush

This isn't to say the *person* is necessarily insubstantial, only that his or her focus may be misplaced.

⁂

This lesson has been one of the harder ones for me to learn, or at least it's taken longer than most. I think many of us who want to be on stage, in leadership positions, or otherwise the center of attention have a certain degree of narcissism: We care too much about how we appear or what others think of us. It can give us the drive and confidence to perform well, but it can also be a blinding force that limits our ability to master our chosen craft.

The key is to be self aware, to find a proper balance, to not lose perspective. Immerse yourself in the things that matter, work passionately toward your goals, strive to be the best leader you can be—and your image will take care of itself.

Food for thought:

- Are you more concerned about your image than the substance of your work?

- When leading your group, what percentage of your focus is on yourself versus the group? How would your team answer that question?

- Is there someone you can check in with from time to time for an objective opinion about whether your focus is well placed?

♮ Life Isn't Fair

I don't think I was ever cut out to teach junior high school, but I'm sure I wasn't ready for it at age twenty-two.[1]

Nevertheless, my career began humbly as a junior high school teacher in Ankeny, Iowa.

After accepting the position of Choral and General Music teacher at the junior high school there, I learned that my predecessor had been a one-year interim appointment after her predecessor landed in prison. It seems he had a thing for junior high boys and invited some of them to his home for some extra-curricular activity. One of the boys eventually told his parents what was going on, and the teacher was convicted of child sex abuse. (Interestingly, I heard a few years later that he had been released from prison and was playing piano in a hotel bar nearby. Seemed like a bad idea to me.)

> [1] *Junior high school is a challenging transitional time for most children, and I think it requires teachers with considerable experience and maturity to succeed there.*

As you might imagine, parents and students alike were scrutinizing me from the first day.

But I made the rounds of the classrooms to drum up some interest in the choirs, volunteered to referee a basketball game, and generally tried (not too hard) to put people's minds at ease.

Apparently it worked because the turnout for the choirs was overwhelming.

On the first day of rehearsal I had set up my classroom expecting about twenty-five interested seventh-graders to show up wanting to join the choir.

By 8:00 that morning 130 students were waiting to sign up.

I talked the custodian into setting up the cafeteria as a temporary rehearsal room, and that's where we ended up for the rest of the year. I felt so happy and relieved that students were willing to trust me so quickly, but with insufficient sheet music, no accompanist, and 130 seventh-graders to manage, the old adage, "Be careful what you wish for," came to mind more than once.

One of those seventh-graders, Bobby, was also in my general music class. Bobby was one of several children from an underprivileged family whose life was difficult in just about every way: His parents didn't offer him much support, he struggled academically, he was physically smaller than most boys his age, and he came to school with a "bowl" haircut and hand-me-down clothes that were too big for him. A few of the other students teased him mercilessly—some children can be so cruel at that age. I always liked Bobby—he was such a nice, kindhearted boy—and I hoped he would make the best of the circumstances life had presented him.

One day, just as I walked into my classroom, I saw Bobby knocking the books off another student's desk. I managed to step in just as the other boy was about to retaliate. I hadn't seen what the other boy did to provoke Bobby's action, but I was sure he had done something.

So I asked Bobby to wait in the hallway, then went to the other boy and said, "I don't know what you did, but whatever it was, don't do it again. Leave Bobby alone." [2]

Then I went out to the hallway to talk to Bobby, who assumed he was in trouble. I assured him he wasn't.

"I just want to talk with you about how to deal with situations like this in the future," I said.

He was on the verge of tears and replied, "Tom is always picking on me, and I'm not going to take it anymore."

[2] *I was picked on similarly when I was in junior high and the early part of high school, so I had a visceral, empathetic reaction to Bobby's situation.*

I told him I understood, but that reacting the way he did was only going to get him into more trouble.

He looked so pitiful and dejected. As he hung his head he said, "The thing is, nobody likes me."

I crouched down in front of him and answered, "Bobby, I just can't believe that. I like you."

"Well, you're the only one," he said through his tears.

Inspiring Harmony

After choking back a few tears of my own, I told Bobby he could visit me anytime he wanted to talk about what was going on in his life, and together we would figure out ways to deal with people who treated him badly without having to get into trouble over it.

After doing his seven weeks in General Music, Bobby moved on in the seventh-grade rotation to Home Economics (what a silly name). As part of that class, students were to cook something and then invite someone special in their lives to come to the class to partake of their culinary creations.

So, Bobby invited me.

He had made pizza, and he was so proud to have me come as his guest. I sat at one of the tables in the classroom, and Bobby brought the pizza to serve me. The problem was, he couldn't get it to come off the spatula, so he finally used his other hand (which obviously hadn't been washed for a while) to slide the pizza onto my plate.

I ate it, of course, telling him how good it was.

And when he asked if I wanted more, you know I had a second piece.

I often wonder what happened to Bobby. Life certainly wasn't fair for him in the seventh grade. Did he overcome the challenges in his life to become a happy and fulfilled adult? I guess I'll never know. As is so often the case, it would have been much easier for him to give in to negative influences, rather than make the effort to climb out of his situation and make a better life.

I'd like to think I gave him at least one reason to feel better about himself and more optimistic about life.

❧ ❧ ❧

As leaders, we are often subjected to unfair criticism, lack of cooperation, and harsh judgment from people who think anyone else could do the job better. It's so hard to avoid feeling indignant, defensive, and hurt, but I've come to learn one can expend a lot of energy fretting about how unfair life can be.

Yes, there is a time to stand up for oneself and to stand up to injustice, but more often, we must find a way to show grace – to sidestep a problem and accept the fact that life simply is not fair.

Food for thought:

- Isn't it frustrating when your well-intentioned efforts on behalf of your group are met with grousing and disapproval? How many coping mechanisms are in your arsenal when such things happen?

- What have you done to help the "Bobby" in your world find understanding and acceptance about life's inequities?

You're Never Too Old

I graduated from the University of Iowa in 1979 with a Bachelor of Music degree, having double-majored in voice and piano, while earning a K-12 teaching certificate. My fiancée and I married one week after graduation, and we moved to Ankeny, Iowa, where I taught general and vocal music in junior high and became a deacon at First Church of Christ.

All was as it should have been, at least in terms of outward appearances.

I conducted the choir at the Ankeny church, which is where I met Bill. Bill didn't sing in the choir—in fact, Bill didn't sing at all.

Like so many others, especially of his generation, Bill had been told by his school music teacher he should stop singing when his voice changed. It was easy to tell, even when I met him at about the age of eighty, that his voice had likely changed overnight. His was a classic case of a boy soprano whose voice suddenly began to mature, and he found himself with some of his high voice remaining, and some new-found low notes that were hard to manage. In between was the great divide, where so many boys find it difficult to phonate (speak or sing) during this sort of voice change—thus the "breaking" or "cracking" we often hear in the voices of young teen boys.[1]

> [1] Significant research has been done in the past fifty years about the changing voice. Voice teachers and choral conductors are generally better educated about how to guide adolescents through this transition than they were when Bill was young. Unfortunately, boys at that time were often told to stop singing (or mouth the words) when the teacher didn't know what else to do. Although less dramatic, girls also experience a changing voice when going through puberty.

Michael Melton

Nearly seventy years later, Bill told me his story.

He said he'd never really felt comfortable singing since this childhood experience. "All I want," he said pleadingly, "is to know I can sing well enough to sing hymns in church without feeling embarrassed. Do you think you could help me?"

The end of the school year was fast approaching, and my only summer job was to be the field announcer for the local high school baseball games, so I agreed to work with Bill during the summer break. We met at the church twice a week, sitting at the piano and reading through hymns. I helped him learn the basics of music reading, and we used all the tricks to help him develop the skills of audiation and pitch-matching.[2]

He had a small vocal range, given his age and the limited use of his voice for so many years, so he learned how to sing an octave lower when the melody went above his usable range. It was a bit of a work-around that made it possible for him to sing along with most hymn tunes. It was fascinating and inspiring to see him so focused on learning this skill, like a child with newfound optimism.

After a few months of working together, near the end of summer, I decided it was time for a "final exam."

> [2] *"Audiation" means being able to hear a pitch in one's mind—what I call "the mind's ear." Then, there is the matter of being able to match that pitch with one's voice—pitch coordination. Many people describe themselves as "tone deaf," when, in fact, they are most often having difficulty with pitch coordination. To varying degrees, pitch coordination can be successfully taught.*

So, I told Bill that at our next meeting, I would hand him a hymn tune he didn't know, play it as I would have for congregational singing, and leave it to him to find his way through the melody of the hymn.

When he arrived for our last session, he was as nervous as a music student about to give a recital—which is, basically, exactly who he was.

We practiced a bit with some familiar tunes to give him a chance to relax and sing through a few melodies.

Then, the final exam.

I pulled out an unfamiliar hymn, asked him to identify the meter and key signature and tell me how he would find his starting pitch. When he was ready, I played an introduction, and he began to sing. He sang through the entire hymn flawlessly and then looked at me anxiously, like a child desperately seeking the approval of a parent or teacher.

I looked him straight in the eye.

"Bill, that was perfect."

Fumbling for his handkerchief, he began to cry. "I can't tell you how much this means to me," he said. "All I ever wanted was to be able to sing hymns in church until I die—and now I know I can."

I put my arm around him and told him how proud of him I was. It's hard to describe how gratifying it was the next Sunday morning to look into the congregation and see Bill singing every hymn joyfully and confidently.

It's sometimes difficult to get out of one's comfort zone and take on a new challenge, especially late in life. For some, that daunting challenge might be to become a leader for the first time. By age eighty, it would have been so much easier for Bill to simply go on week after week and year after year, accepting what he had been told as a child: "… you should stop singing." But how much richer were the last years of his life because he found the courage to face his fear, ask for some assistance, and overcome this nearly lifelong obstacle.

How fortunate for him, and for me, that he decided he wasn't too old.

Food for thought:

- Is there something in life you've always wished you had done? Maybe it isn't too late …

- Is there a group that could use your leadership, but you've been reluctant to take the plunge?

- Are there older people in your group who need your encouragement to stay active or try something new?

Michael Melton

ⓗ Choose Your Battles Wisely

It's one of the most frequently offered bits of advice, yet one of the most difficult to follow.

We can often see when a conflict is likely unresolvable or, at the very least, will cost more time and energy than it's worth. And yet we just can't seem to walk away.

What is it that drives us to engage? The need to be right? The need to win? The need to prove a point? Or do some of us feed off the (negative) energy that comes from conflict?

The question I've learned to ask myself when faced with conflict is, "How would I like this to end?"

Often there isn't a completely satisfying outcome, but there is usually a solution that seems better than others—or at least a path of least resistance. Everyone in a position of leadership or authority should learn this lesson at some point. I say they should, but I'm sure we can all think of leaders who seem not to have figured it out after years of locking horns.

For many, the lesson is learned through parenting. Lord knows, if a parent chooses to fight every battle that presents itself with a child, constant misery—for all involved—is inevitable.

Similarly, classroom teachers, business leaders, anyone responsible for leading or simply working with others, needs to ask these important questions:

- "What are the potential consequences if I choose to fight this battle?"
- "If I engage in this particular conflict, will I be less effective when a more important one arises?"

Inspiring Harmony

- "In the end, will the outcome of this disagreement really matter?"

Maybe it's the need to save face that drives us to engage. *I'm not going to sit still and take that*, I can hear myself say.

So we rise up, ready to fight, before taking a moment to consider the possible outcomes.

Another very important question to ask is, "How will this affect my relationship with the other person/people in the future?"

"Winning the battle and losing the war" can be a high price to pay.

The most successful negotiators seem to be the ones who know how to come away with a deal or solution that allows the other party to save face. There's nothing quite like getting what you want and letting the other person think it was his or her idea. What a shame our elected political leaders have lost sight of this important concept: The art of compromise to serve the best interest of the people has, unfortunately, given way to polarizing extremism.[1]

> [1] This is one of the greatest threats to American society today. As we retreat ever further left and right, becoming increasingly dogmatic in our beliefs, our ability to "promote the general welfare" is ever diminished.

As I mentioned in the previous chapter, my first church choir after graduating from the University of Iowa was at First Church of Christ in Ankeny, Iowa. I was twenty-two years old and had some big ideas, so I would occasionally program music that was a bit esoteric—not always to the liking of some members of the choir or the congregation.

During one choir rehearsal, one of the sopranos remarked, "Where did you find this song? What a terrible piece!"

Without pause, I fired back at her, "This is an excellent new composition. I've studied this and should know better than you."

Needless to say, the rest of the rehearsal was awkward, and there was tension between that singer and me for several months thereafter.

Should she have made that comment, particularly during a choir rehearsal?

No.

Should I have found a more mature way to respond?

Absolutely.

It could well have been a moment for teaching, or even humor, rather than the beginning of a contentious few months. In the long run, her comment would have been forgotten and my righteous indignation would have passed.

Instead, it took much too long for tensions to relax and peace to be restored.

I must have learned something over the next few years. My next church position was in the Chicago area at Immanuel United Church of Christ in Evergreen Park, Illinois. Much could be said about the interesting personalities there, but I fondly remember a particular tenor named Robert Mueller.

Bob was a physical education teacher at the local high school and sang with a barbershop group. His musical tastes were clearly and narrowly defined, and he certainly had no use for anything sung in a foreign language. It should also be noted that Bob became a little hard of hearing as he aged, so he sometimes spoke more loudly than he realized.

Anyway, I often brought out anthems by the world's great composers and usually insisted that we sing them in their original languages, printing a translation in the church bulletin.

At one rehearsal when we were singing a motet [2] in Latin, Bob leaned over to the man next to him and said a little too loudly, "Well, you can sure see why this is a dead language."

[2] The term "motet" has been used broadly and is therefore difficult to specifically define. It generally refers to music to be sung by multiple voice parts, usually a cappella, and on a sacred text.

I remembered how quickly and vociferously I had defended my musical choice a few years earlier and decided to just let it go.

Interestingly, as I looked at the rest of the choir, there were several knowing smiles that as much as said, *I heard that, and I know you heard that, and best to let it go, and, actually, it was pretty funny, wasn't it ...*

It can be so hard sometimes to take a deep breath and let things go. And certainly there are times when the battle should be fought, when the outcome matters enough to "fall on your sword."

To choose those battles wisely can be an elusive skill, however—one which requires self-awareness and the ability to take a step back in an instant to see the bigger picture before launching. It's a lesson I've learned, but a skill I still struggle to perfect.

As a leader, save your energy for the battles that really matter. Others will admire your restraint, and you will come to enjoy the sense of contentment that follows.

Food for thought:

- Is it time for you to let go of a battle that just is not worth the fight?

- As discussed in the chapter "Life Isn't Fair," how adept are you at sidestepping minor jabs and slights, while saving your political capital for more important issues?

- Look for opportunities to practice the discipline of self-restraint—make a game of it. With practice, it becomes easier and even satisfying.

Michael Melton

(h) There's More Than One Way

In 1982 I moved to Chicago to become the Music Director of the Chicago Children's Choir (CCC). I was twenty-five years old at the time, and, with all of two years teaching experience and a freshly minted master's degree, I was ready to hit the ground running.

Mike at the Chicago Children's Choir

The CCC had a noble history and mission, envisioned and guided by the late Christopher Moore since 1956, the year I was born. Chris was a passionate firebrand, as interested in social justice as in choral experiences for children. He was given a sabbatical the same year I was hired, and the board's intention was to reorganize the Choir in his absence.

The CCC had grown to include about 600 children in various choirs and programs by then, and it was indeed time to make some changes. But to take a leadership role in such a challenging project would require not merely a good musician and conductor, but a person of considerable experience, insight, and maturity.

Unfortunately, in 1982, that wasn't me.

The Choir employed several other musical staff at the time, including three other main conductors: Martha Swisher, Keith Hampton, and Nick Page. Each one brought unique skills and talents to the Choir.

Inspiring Harmony

Martha was an excellent voice teacher and coach, and the children loved her. I remember observing her with a group of upper elementary students rehearsing "O Holy Night," the Christmas song composed by Adolphe Adam.

As the energy in the room reached a high pitch, she stopped the group to make a comment and then turned away as she thought about where to restart the piece.

Christopher Moore

"Fall on your knees," she said, intending to restart at the beginning of the first chorus. (The chorus begins with the words "Fall on your knees.")

When she turned back to face the group, the children were all dutifully on their knees, ready to sing.

Keith had an infectious enthusiasm for music and life. He was a superb musician and organist with a strong academic background. Although well versed in most musical styles from the time I met him, he has since become particularly effective when leading gospel music. He also taught music theory and helped develop training materials for the choirs of the CCC to use.

Martha Swisher

Nick was always "of the people." Easy going, self-effacing, and genial, he was a wonderful person to have as a friend. He also enjoyed composing and arranging and was very skilled at it—often inspired. He was a great fit for that choir, both musically and socially.

With such a multi-talented group of conductors, not to mention a strong musical and administrative staff, my job as Music Director should have been to harness all that energy to effect positive changes and a forward-looking new vision for the Choir.

I'm afraid I instead waltzed in presuming to have all the answers and made sure everyone knew it. Part of my behavior was defensive and undoubtedly sprang from the fact that my marriage of only three years was about to end—my wife and baby daughter, Emily, moved from Iowa City to St. Louis while I went to Chicago.

Nonetheless, life would have been so much easier if I could have had the courage to embrace what others had to offer, rather than alienating them.

Although I regretted each damaged relationship in some way, I felt most badly about Chris. When he returned from his sabbatical, distressed about what had happened in his absence, instead of finding a way to build on the legacy he had created, I actually told him I didn't think he was qualified to conduct a professional children's choir.

Why would I say that?!

It's true, his choral rehearsal and conducting techniques lacked skill and finesse.

But the question I ask myself now is: Who cares?!

As its founder, Chris had knowledge of the choir, its repertoire, and its history.

That deserved to be celebrated, and I failed to embrace it.[1]

Keith Hampton

> [1] *This book is a compilation of lessons I've learned from things I did well or things I did poorly. This is definitely an instance of coming up short.*

To think your way is the only way is the height of arrogance. Teachers, leaders, and performers are so committed to their techniques, their processes, and their beliefs, that it's easy for them to think their way is the best—or even the only way.

No matter how skilled and talented you may be, others have been there before you, and others will

Inspiring Harmony

come after. Better to learn from those who have come before and those with whom you now work—to share ideas as a team and inspire harmony among your colleagues.

And remember, there is always more than one way …

Food for thought:

- Who are the people in your life from whom you could learn?

- If someone else, say a co-leader, chooses a different process from what you may think is best for your group, are you willing to support that person in his or her efforts?

- Can you think of a technique in your area of expertise that you once thought was sacrosanct, only to later realize there were other, perhaps better ways?

Michael Melton

🎵 Walk a Mile in My Shoes

I can't hear that expression without thinking of Eric, a particularly talented eighth-grader who was always coming up with witty comments—and he had great timing. He was in my junior high general music class in 1979.

That was the year I decided to use popular music to discuss the underlying meaning of song lyrics and the ways in which music enhances text. We were listening to Elvis Presley's "Walk a Mile in My Shoes."

I asked, "What does it mean to walk a mile in someone else's shoes? What is the subtext, the deeper meaning of the words?"

Eric raised his hand and, with a grin he couldn't hide, answered, "The agony of de-feet." I love that sort of clever humor!

My more poignant memory is of being in a rehearsal with the Chicago Children's Choir (CCC) in January 1983 celebrating the birthday of Rev. Dr. Martin Luther King, Jr.

President Ronald Reagan had signed the bill that same year making King's birthday (actually January 15th, but celebrated the third Monday in January) an official holiday that would be first observed three years later. We were taking time out of a Saturday morning rehearsal to reflect on the life of the great civil rights leader.

Rev. Dr. Martin Luther King, Jr.

Inspiring Harmony

But before I continue, a little background: I grew up in a part of Illinois that was slow to come to terms with the idea of diversity. I remember having an older cousin who dated a man who was a part-time Baptist minister and, I'm quite certain, a KKK member. He would never admit to it because he always said, "I couldn't tell you even if I were."

"I think you're a coward," I told him. "If you feel so strongly about your bigoted and racist ideas as to be a member of the Klan, at least have the courage to say it out loud." [1]

> [1] My language was actually more colorful, but I've chosen not to include it verbatim here.

The town of Carterville, where I lived from ages eight to nineteen, was all white, so far as I knew, and had only one Jewish family, so far as I knew. The story, as was told to me, was that three African-American families had tried to move to Carterville at different times, and all three were burned out of their homes. In one of those cases, a member of our church who was a mechanic heard that the town's fire truck wouldn't start, so he went to the firehouse to help get it started. When he was told his services were not required, he insisted he could help—but was told in no uncertain terms he should move on and not get involved.

I also recall a time when my father, the minister of our church, invited an African-American student from Southern Illinois University to share with our congregation the story of his father's work in Chicago. He announced the upcoming visit during a Sunday morning service. One of the older congregants, Bess, was livid at the idea, stormed to the back of the sanctuary afterward and declared to my father, "It'll be over my dead body that a nigger ever stands in that pulpit."

My father's response was, "Well, Bess, I didn't realize you'd be leaving us so soon—he'll be here next week."

Mike conducting the Chicago Children's Choir in 1983 at the inauguration of Harold Washington, the first African-American mayor of Chicago

She was even more incensed at his retort, but she was back in her pew the next week anyway.

I had only seen a black person a few times during my childhood, and only touched a black person once that I can recall, shaking the hand of a black minister. Of course, after leaving high school, I encountered many people of different races and ethnicities, but when I went to Chicago and the CCC, I was suddenly faced with a room full of children where half of the faces were black.

Back to that Saturday morning …

As the staff took turns telling where they were when King was assassinated, I decided to tell the story of where I grew up. As the story unfolded, I looked around the room to see every eye riveted on me, as if in disbelief.

Then came the crushing realization that I had never before told this story to a black person.

I felt so overwhelmed with sadness, I had to leave the room without finishing my story. Some of the older children were thoughtful and caring enough to leave the rehearsal after a few minutes to see if I was OK.

After composing myself, I went back and explained to the group that it was, in fact, the first time I had told my story to a black person, and to see all those young, innocent faces was unexpectedly moving for me.

The experience provided a new layer of meaning to me of what it means to walk a mile in someone else's shoes. I knew what I had witnessed as a child was horribly wrong, but I don't think I had any true sympathy for the victims until I put actual faces on it. I couldn't help thinking how there may have been children just like the ones in the Choir who lost their homes to racial violence in the town where I was raised.

I hadn't actually walked a mile in their shoes, having never been the victim of racial discrimination myself, but I certainly could empathize more with those who had by putting a face on what I had witnessed as a child. I learned an important lesson about leading with grace: The most effective leaders seek ways to understand and connect with others—to absorb their life's experience—to walk a mile in their shoes.

Inspiring Harmony

Food for thought:

- What life experiences have shaped your thinking and behavior? Might that help explain how others perceive you?

- Who in your life deserves your better understanding?

- If there is someone in your organization with whom you are having difficulty, consider what life experiences may have shaped his or her thinking and behavior. How will you approach them differently in the future?

Michael Melton

Leaders Must Have Thick Skin

I sang with the Chicago Symphony Chorus from 1982 to 1989 with its founding director, Margaret Hillis. Miss Hillis was not an easy person to get to know, but having spent five of those years as a tenor section leader, I got a glimpse into her personality, her work ethic, and her vulnerabilities.

Like many female conductors even today, Miss Hillis had to prove herself time and again.[1]

Over the years, she developed a number of coping mechanisms and some pretty thick skin.

One season, an inordinate number of choristers (there are always some) were making negative comments about Miss Hillis behind her back. (Interesting how easy it is to malign another person when the target of your barbs is out of earshot.) She became aware of the criticism, as is usually the case, but didn't address it in front of the full Chorus until one evening when a rehearsal got a little uncomfortable. Things were not going particularly well that night, and some singers felt emboldened to voice criticism of her in ways that were hard to ignore.

> [1] *Conducting (especially orchestral conducting) has long been a male-dominated field. That has certainly changed in recent years, particularly in the choral field, but biases remain.*

Her only comment was to the Chorus in general, "Things look very different from this side of the music stand."

I've told my conducting students that story many times when we've had discussions about the characteristics of a good leader. One important trait is, you must have thick skin.

My last position as a church music director was at the Community Church of Wilmette, Illinois.

Inspiring Harmony

My family and I were actually members of that church before I was asked to serve as its music director, and I was at first reluctant to accept the position, knowing some of the history of the church and its music program. Four paid soloists (three of whom were also church members) had exercised considerable control over decisions made concerning the choir for a long time.

It didn't help matters that the church decided to stop paying those soloists in order to fund the new music director position they were creating for me. It set up quite an antagonistic relationship between the soloists and me, as well as the members of the church who were aligned with them.

Although leaders of the church assured me I would be supported during what would undoubtedly be a difficult transition, things quickly went from bad to worse. Halfway through my first year, I attended a music committee meeting where the usual issues were being thrashed about yet again, and I asked the committee what they thought was at the heart of the antagonism we were all feeling.

Margaret Hillis onstage at Orchestra Hall in Chicago, 1979 (Jim Steere photo, courtesy of the Chicago Symphony Orchestra's Rosenthal Archives)

One of the committee members, the wife of one of the soloists, answered, "The problem isn't with the program; the problem is you."

I was ready to throw in the towel by the end of that first year, but decided I really should follow through on my commitment and help see the music program through this difficult time.[2]

That's not an easy thing to do when you know very well you will have to continue working with people who don't like you, don't want you there, and think you're fouling up absolutely everything.

> [2] *My contract with the church was only a year at a time, but I felt I had made a commitment to help the church change the structure of its music program and chose not to resign after only one year.*

I stayed in the position for five years, and when I resigned the directorship, I also left the church.

Consider the many ways of coping with situations where your efforts as a leader are thwarted and your integrity is questioned. The knee-jerk reaction, to be defensive and argumentative, is usually the least effective. But to roll over and play dead won't solve anything either.

One of the lessons I've learned over the years, including through my experience with Community Church, is that it's not always best to meet a problem head on and see if you can bulldoze your way through it. As with "choosing your battles wisely," ask yourself instead:

"How would I like to see this end?"

"Does it make more sense to go around this obstacle, rather than through it?"

"Can I change the perception and the intention of the person with whom I have an issue such that they will choose to be my friend, rather than my enemy?"

The happy outcome could be, instead of a winner and a loser, the conflict is simply resolved. Unfortunately, it's one of the lessons that has taken me a while to learn.

Standing in front of a group of people, knowing that at least some of them don't like you, or think you're failing at your task, or simply think you're the wrong person for the job, takes enormous courage.

One method I use to deal with that is to imagine those particular people as children. Seeing individuals as they must have been as children opens a window into what they've become as adults. Were they popular, pretty, smart, overweight, short, shy, a bully, the victim of a bully?

Seeing people as they must have been as children encourages a certain sympathy, or even empathy, for those whose behavior can seem callous and hurtful.[3]

> [3] *This is an interesting exercise. If you have an opportunity to see photos or videos or even hear descriptions of adult members of your group from when they were children, pay attention. You can learn so much about the adults you lead by seeing them as children.*

I believe most people do not intend to be hurtful, and a good leader must learn to accept that. It also helps to remember, alongside the vocal minority of complainers sits the generally silent majority of happy campers.

※ ※ ※

Some of us seem to have an innate proclivity for leadership, but we must be prepared for inevitable, demoralizing criticism.

If you aspire to become president of the United States, you should understand that, at any given moment, half the country or more will think you're the wrong person for the job. To abide such withering criticism and continue to lead with optimism requires considerable grace.

To survive as a political or business leader, teacher, or conductor, one must develop thick skin.

Food for thought:

- Have you learned the fine art of rolling with the punches?

- Are you able to take helpful suggestions to heart, while letting empty criticism go by?

- Do you sincerely invite members of your group to offer comments and suggestions? Do they think your invitation is sincere?

Michael Melton

♭ Admit Your Mistakes

Everyone would like to be spared the embarrassment that mistakes can sometimes bring, but it's usually so much easier to simply face them with grace and, often, with a dash of self-effacing humor. Trying to cover oneself by making contrived explanations is pointless—most people will see through them anyway.

With your indulgence, this chapter will be my opportunity for confession.

During my first few years of singing with the Chicago Symphony Chorus, I was privileged to work with a talented quintet of singers called "The Singayres." I sang a bit with the group but mostly served as its accompanist and coach.

We performed for private functions and, in our second year of existence, made a Christmas recording.

I was helping edit the

"The Singayres"
Christmas recording flyer

LIGHT UP your **CHRISTMAS** $7.95
SHARE THE CHRISTMAS SPIRIT

Give the gift of song for office parties, stocking stuffers, party atmosphere, grab bags, teachers, family, & friends!

BRIGHT holiday songs and Christmas carols
WARM mellow sounds of close vocal harmonies
COLORFUL a cappella Christmas cheer
Chicago's top professionals: The SINGAYRES

Inspiring Harmony

[1] *Louis "Studs" Terkel was a Chicago institution with an illustrious life and career, much too rich to describe in detail in this limited space. He was an actor, activist, historian, author, and radio broadcaster.*
According to the WFMT radio website working to archive his contributions, he devoted forty-five years to WFMT—9,000+ hours of radio and book interviews and 5,000+ hours of "unique voices and stories."

Studs Terkel interviewed Christopher Moore, Founding Director of the Chicago Children's Choir, on his program in 1979.

Mahalia Jackson

recording at WFMT studios (the classical music radio station in Chicago) when I ran into Louis "Studs" Terkel.[1]

I had met Studs while conducting the Chicago Children's Choir, and he remembered me (as he did pretty much everyone he ever met). When I told him I was editing a new recording, he invited me on the spot to be a guest on his WFMT interview show to talk about it.

I was to be the only guest on his hour-long program, and there was no script; he would simply sit with his guests and talk for an hour. He was so well versed on so many subjects it was astounding.

We discussed and played tracks from the recording, and when we came to the song "I Wonder as I Wander," he called his producer into the booth and said, "I did an interview with Mahalia

54

Jackson, and she sang this song—see if you can find that and we'll play it." [2]

And after a minute, he called the producer back, "I also interviewed John Jacob Niles, and he sang it, accompanying himself on the dulcimer—see if you can find that one, also." [3]

So, after hearing my group's rendition, we heard Mahalia Jackson and John Jacob Niles perform "I Wonder as I Wander." An incredible experience …

Later in the program, we were discussing an arrangement by Ralph Vaughan Williams, which we were about to play. While introducing the piece, I pronounced the composer's name "Ralph," as it is commonly pronounced in America, rather than "Rafe," as Vaughan Williams pronounced it, and as it is commonly pronounced in Britain. When Studs began playing the recording, I was kicking myself for having made such a blunder.

"May we please go back and record that again?" I asked.

"No, we only record live to tape," he responded. "There is no editing here."

"But I really would like to fix my mistake," I pleaded. "Anyone who hears this is going to notice what I did."

"If that's the biggest mistake you ever make," he said with a smile, "you'll be fine."

He was, of course, right to let such a minor mistake pass, and he was very gracious in the way he handled it.

And now, for my second confession … I've spent several years score reading for the Ravinia Festival, [4] summer home of the Chicago Symphony Orchestra. There are large video screens either

> [2] Mahalia Jackson, a powerful singer and civil rights activist, was known as "The Queen of Gospel." It was a thrill, but also intimidating to have her recording played directly after mine.

John Jacob Niles

> [3] John Jacob Niles was best known as a collector of traditional American ballads. His composition, "I Wonder as I Wander," based on melodic fragments he heard sung by Annie Morgan, a young girl in Murphy, North Carolina, has been frequently performed by vocal and choral ensembles for decades.

Inspiring Harmony

> [4] The Ravinia Festival is the oldest outdoor music festival in the United States. It has been the summer home of the Chicago Symphony Orchestra since 1936 and hosts world-class artists from nearly every musical genre.

side of the Pavilion stage, and a camera crew shoots the concerts so the audience can see the performers up close and personal. (This is known as an IMAG production—short for "Image Magnification.")

With most small music groups, the video director can "wing it" and manage to put a good show on the screens. But with an orchestra, the director and camera crew need some help figuring out who's playing next and which instrument(s) are most important at any given moment. That's where the score reader comes in. (A more complete "score reader" job description comes in the chapter titled "Suck It Up.")

It's quite a challenge, but a lot of fun.

In July 2012, the CSO was playing Mahler's Symphony #6 ("Tragic"), where there are famous moments in the finale known as the "hammer blows." A percussionist raises a very large mallet that looks something like a wooden sledgehammer and slams it down on a wooden box, in a manner prescribed by Mahler as "short and powerful, but heavy and dull and with a non-metallic character (like the stroke of an axe)." [5]

Cynthia Yeh, Chicago Symphony Orchestra principal percussionist, wielding the "Mahler hammer."

What a perfect moment for those large video screens! The problem was, I didn't know about the hammer blow. Somehow, I had managed to prepare the score without discovering it, and I had never heard of it before, so we had something else on the screens during the most dramatic visual moment in the entire symphony. After the performance, several people (including one of the security guards!)

asked me why we didn't get the hammer blow on the screens. *How many other audience members*, I wondered, *were on the edge of their seats waiting for the big moment?*

I made some excuse about "technical difficulties," but the truth is, I didn't know about it. I just couldn't bring myself to admit to that at the time, and I'm not sure it would have mattered much if I had, but at least my confession is out there now.

Although, frankly, that doesn't make me feel any better about it.

> [5] *There were actually three hammer blows added by Mahler to his original score—some even say five. It is an interesting story and study why he reduced it to two in 1906 after conducting the première. Some conductors use only one hammer blow, some use two, and a few (most notably Leonard Bernstein) have reinstated the third blow.*

The real question is, why is it so difficult to simply admit a mistake? Are we afraid of losing the respect of others because we may not know something they or we think we should? Are we afraid we will be diminished in the eyes of others as professionals? Or do some of us have such a perfectionist streak that mistakes simply aren't allowed?

For many leaders, far too much energy is wasted trying to keep up appearances. And we risk losing our credibility if we persist in trying to cover up our mistakes.

So, admit them.

(For further discussion about mistakes, see the chapter titled "First, Land the Airplane.")

❦ ❦ ❦

As I say to my students, "If you find you've made a mistake, get in line behind the rest of us."

We all do it, and I believe others will respect you and even admire you more if you own up to your mistakes and then let them go.

The attribute of strong leaders is not that they never falter, but that they are genuine.

Food for thought:

- Can you remember a time when you publicly admitted a mistake and then let it go? It didn't hurt much, did it …

- Do the members of your team feel comfortable admitting their mistakes? If not, why not?

- What can you do to make your organization a place where mistakes are acknowledged and corrected as necessary, without fear?

Michael Melton

♭ Never Settle for Mezzo Beige

I was fortunate to have had the opportunity to sing for many of the world's greatest conductors during the 1980s and early '90s. I learned a great deal from watching them work and trying to build a mental catalog of the techniques I thought were effective, or not. I sometimes sang from a full score (the entire work, including orchestration, rather than the vocal parts only), just so I could see what the conductor was seeing—which happened to prompt a "Grant Park Symphony Chorus Violation" one summer.

A few members of this Chicago chorus had compiled a very funny list of things some chorus members do (pretending to lapse into a foreign language without intending to, laughing too much at the conductor's jokes, and bringing a full score to rehearsals, among many "transgressions"). Nevertheless, it was wonderful to be paid to sing some of the

Sir Georg Solti,
© BBC Photo Library

Inspiring Harmony

Grant Park Symphony Chorus
REHEARSAL POLICE
SUMMONS

NAME OF OFFENDER: **MELTON**

VOCAL OFFENSES	FINE
Obtrusive Vocal Technique	$20.00
Unsuccessful Pitch Approximation	$10.00
Any Hint of Countertenor Singing	$15.00
Snoring	$20.00
Snoring while Singing	$50.00
Eerie Vocal Similarity to:	
Elmer Fudd	$25.00
Bert Lahr	$25.00
Natural Disasters	$25.00
Death Screams (not in score)	$50.00
Obstruction of Diction	$25.00
Ungodly Noises (Musical)	$25.00
Failure to Negotiate Register Breaks	$15.00
Grotesque Facial Expressions While Singing	$30.00

IMPERSONATING A PROFESSIONAL	
Stupid Questions	$10.00
Really Stupid Questions	$25.00
Really Stupid Questions which Increase Rehearsal Length	$300.00

Presumptuous First Year Behavior	
Musicology	$25.00
Historical Nitpicking	$50.00
Use of Tape Recorder	$25.00
Endless Diction Questions	$100.00
Obtrusive Foot Tapping	$10.00
☒ Uninvited Conducting	$15.00

General Toadying	
☒ Insane Cackling at Conductors' Bad Jokes	$50.00
Unwarranted Beatific Smiling While Singing	$40.00
☒ Conspicuous Professional Reading (e.g. Opera News, etc.)	$35.00
Stultifyingly Minute Vocal Technique Questions	$75.00
Conversing with Conductor in Language other than English	$95.00
Conspicuous Score Marking	$15.00
Violent Nodding	$25.00
Obvious, Insipid Score Study During Breaks	$50.00
Affected Artfulness in Rhythmic Reading	$60.00
Obsequiously Erect Posture	$50.00

☒ Warming up during Rehearsal	$35.00
Singing Full Voice in the Front Row	$50.00
Raising Hand after Making Mistake	$40.00
References to Obscure Recordings/Performances	$90.00
☒ Pretending to Understand Absurd Metaphor	$15.00
☒ Actually Understanding Absurd Metaphor	$25.00

Annoying Behavior by Veterans	
Singing High Notes Louder than Possible	$25.00
Holding Same ¼ beat Longer than Everyone Else	$200.00
Failing to Mark	$30.00
Marking all but High Notes	$50.00
Singing Unassigned Solo Parts (sotto voce)	$25.00
Singing Unassigned Solo Parts (fortissimo)	$100.00
Obvious use of Beverages for Vocal Purposes	$75.00
Discussing Vocal Technique during Rehearsal	$100.00
Discussing Vocal Technique during Break	$500.00

Roadmapping:		
	Irrational	$20.00
	Random	$30.00
	Transsexual	$50.00

Feigning European Birth by "Lapsing" into Foreign Language		$100.00
Tiresome Time-Consuming Anecdotes		$30.00
☒ Bringing the Full Score	BELATED PREVIOUS	$25.00
Naming Yourself after an Opera	YEARS	$900.00

CRIMINAL BAD TASTE	
Decomposing	$25.00
Offensive Fragrances	$35.00
Selling Amway Products	$500.00
Absurd Fashion Statements	$50.00
☒ Having Entirely Too Much Fun	$10.00
Chorus Interruptus	$50.00

☐ OTHER:

© 1991, The Boys in the Back Row

greatest music in the world and get a conducting lesson with every rehearsal and concert. It was better training than any book or class could ever offer.

The conductor with whom I sang the most was Sir Georg Solti when he was music director of the Chicago Symphony Orchestra. Solti had seemingly endless energy for life and for music. Everything he did, from conducting to coaching to simply walking the hallway, was at high speed and with great determination and intensity. He was mostly bald, with only a rim of hair—which explains why the stage crew at Orchestra Hall in Chicago used to call him "the screaming skull." That intensity was never stronger than when he was on the podium.

I recall a Chicago Symphony Chorus rehearsal in which Solti felt he wasn't getting enough energy from the singers. At one point, he literally leapt off the podium (he was in his mid-70s at the time), ran back and forth in front of the first row of singers and screamed, "Why don't you have more energy? Look at me—I'm older than all of you, and I have more energy than all of you combined!"

Solti's intensity was fairly unbridled on the podium. Although his gestures were severe, his musicianship was always evident. What was most striking to me was that not a single musical moment was ever thrown away. There was never the sense that the chorus or the orchestra was merely coasting along waiting for something exciting to happen. Instead, Solti drew the most out of every note and every phrase.

It was as if he was saying, *Life is too short to waste even a second. Make the most of every moment.*

His range of musical expression, whether with dynamics, tempi, articulation, or phrasing was always extremely broad.

What I learned from many great conductors is: Mediocrity is a dreadful way to squander one's life.

My favorite line when a chorus or orchestra I'm conducting is being lazy is, "If it's going to be mezzo beige, why bother?" I like the combined image of mezzo (Italian for "half") and beige (the epitome of "neutral"). It's about as "blah" as I can imagine.

What I learned from Solti is to make music as descriptive as possible. If the dynamic contrast is forte to piano, make it bigger than life. If the phrase is sweeping or soaring, pull every ounce of emotion from it. Music is so much more satisfying for both the performers and the audience when it is descriptive.

Is music then programmatic?

> [1] *The ongoing debate concerns whether music can be programmatic. "Program music" is said to be representational, depicting or at least suggesting something extra-musical—a story, a scene, a work of art. "Absolute music" is abstract, representing nothing in particular. Some who question whether music can be specifically programmatic point to Aaron Copland's* Appalachian Spring, *composed without a title, except for "Ballet for Martha" (it was composed for Martha Graham). Graham suggested the title* Appalachian Spring *after a Hart Crane poem where "spring" actually meant a water source. Copland was amused at the number of people who commented on how perfectly he captured the essence of springtime in Appalachia.*
> *Oh, the power of suggestion.*

> [2] *I heard this story secondhand from my brother Mark, so I can't vouch for all the details. But its message is clear and has stuck with me for many years.*

That's a debate for another book. But it certainly is a language that cries out for dramatic expression. [1]

Music and art are metaphors for life. I realize every day cannot be a continuous "mountaintop" experience, but why should it be perpetually dull? Why not find reasons and ways to punch it up as often as possible? Why not make time to do the things we love—and do them with positive energy and passion? Why not be the leader who inspires harmony?

Merely marking time, hoping and planning for the days when you'll actually enjoy life seems so misguided.

As John Lennon said, "Life is what happens to you while you're making other plans."

I knew of a man who graduated from high school, married his high school sweetheart, and took a job at the local factory. [2] He didn't really want to work at the factory—his passion was for woodworking—but he thought he needed to provide a stable income, and the factory seemed the surest way to do that.

As he got promotions and raises over the years, he continued to think he couldn't afford to quit and pursue his dream, so he just kept going to the factory.

Finally, at age fifty-nine, he reached a breaking point and declared to his wife, "I just can't take it one more day."

She replied, "If that's how you feel, you should quit your job and do what you really want to do."

So, one year before being eligible for retirement, he quit his job and began creating wood pieces.

Six months later, he died.

Friends asked his wife if she wished he had continued at the factory until retirement; she lost a lot of his retirement money because he quit early.

"Not at all," she replied. "He was never so happy as during the last six months of his life, and I wouldn't trade that for anything."

It's so sad he waited so long to do what he truly loved.

Mike with his brother, Mark

Life is short—who knows how short.

To waste it by marking time or settling for whatever may come easily is to dull our senses. To enthusiastically pursue a passion, to make the most of a leadership opportunity, is to experience life to the fullest, to wring out all the joy life has to offer. Make the most of your music, your art, your woodworking, your dream, whatever that may be.

And never, ever settle for mezzo beige!

Food for thought

- Do you find ways every day to break free of the mundane?
- Do you motivate your group to expand its horizons and reach beyond its usual boundaries?
- Do you find it exciting to take risks?

♭h) Making Music Is Healing

In 1988 I was singing with the Chicago Symphony Chorus when Sir Georg Solti made a recording of the *St. Matthew Passion* by Johann Sebastian Bach.[1] The forces were formidable: Kiri Te Kanawa, Anne Sofie von Otter, Anthony Rolfe Johnson, Tom Krause, Hans Peter Blochwitz, the Glen Ellyn Children's Chorus, and the Chicago Symphony Orchestra and Chorus.

An inordinate amount of rehearsal time was set aside for chorus preparation, and we gave four performances before the recording was made.

The rehearsal process was meticulous to the point of being painful. Anyone who sang with Margaret Hillis, the founding director of the Chicago Symphony Chorus, knows how attentive to detail she always was. Nevertheless, after weeks of preparation, Solti came to his first Conductor's Piano Rehearsal and was not pleased, particularly with the soprano and tenor sections. I happened to be a tenor section leader at the time, so I was feeling a bit on the hot seat. Solti was so keen to make a superior recording of this epic work, he insisted on hearing every chorus soprano and tenor individually.

So, we were all summoned to Orchestra Hall and, one after the next, walked onto the stage with only our accompanist, Bettie, and a piano to greet us, and sang excerpts from *St. Matthew*. I don't recall the outcome of the soprano hearings, but nearly half of the tenor section was replaced. The singers' union objected to this breach of contract, but Solti got what he wanted anyway.

---

[1] I believe Bach's *St. Matthew Passion is the greatest musical drama ever written. It is massive in scope with carefully selected texts exquisitely set to music—a most beautiful and moving work.*

Michael Melton

At the concerts I stood next to Christopher, another tenor and Miss Hillis' personal assistant at the time. The performances were beautiful—the fruits of our labors were evident. At one of the concerts, the performance of "O Haupt voll Blut und Wunden" [2] was particularly powerful.

The silence when the music ended was spellbinding, and, as the chorus sat, Chris leaned over to me and whispered, "And that's why we do this."

I nodded in agreement.

When the entire three-hour performance ended, Solti had to pause and wipe a tear before he began the bows. It was a moving experience for the audience and performers alike.

But music is more than moving; it's also healing. The choirs I conducted at Northeastern Illinois University (NEIU) from 1996 to 2013 included community residents who volunteered their time to sing with the students. One of my favorite volunteers was a tenor named Dennis Burmeister—a man in his sixties, of slight build, and always with neatly combed gray hair. Dennis attended a choral concert early in my tenure at NEIU. I'm sure it wasn't a stellar performance, but he really wanted to sing and came to me afterward

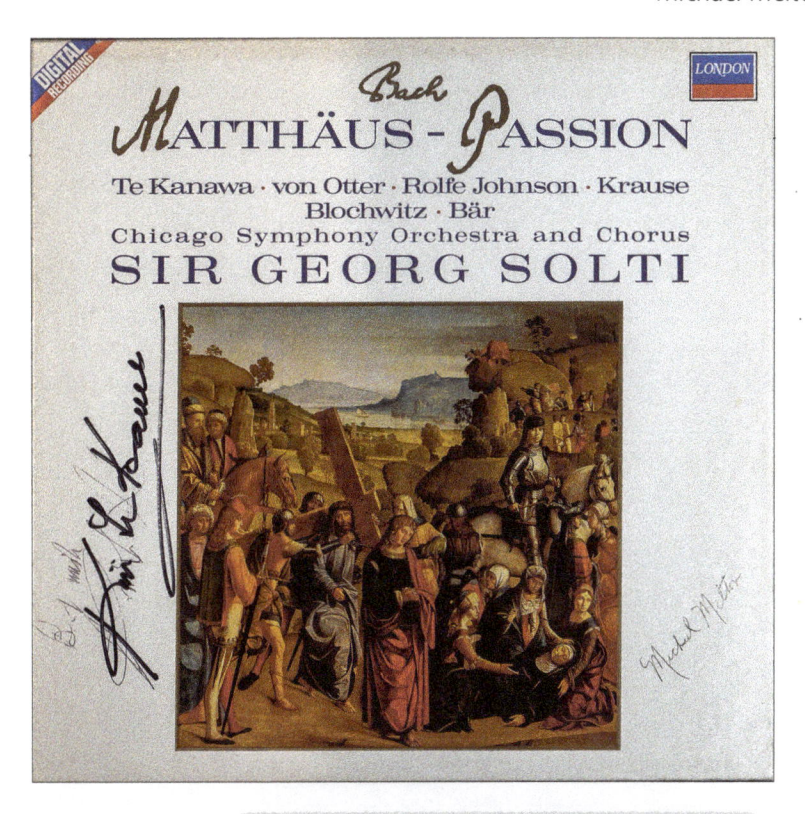

[2] *This is perhaps the most famous chorale from* St. Matthew. *Most English-speaking people know it as "O Sacred Head."*
The translation of the first verse is:
O Head full of blood and wounds,
full of pain and full of derision,
O Head, in mockery bound
with a crown of thorns,
O Head, once beautifully adorned
with the most honor and adornment,
but now most dishonored:
let me greet you!

to ask about joining the choirs. I was begging for singers to join us, particularly tenors, so I was happy to have such an enthusiastic singer come on board.

Dennis not only loved music, great singers in particular, but he seemed to need a way to express and release his emotions. He was wrapped a little tightly—disappointed if the ensemble wasn't singing well and excited if it was. What I remember best were his reactions to those many moments in music that give us all goose bumps. I say "all," but I suppose that isn't really true. Some of us just seem to have more sensitivity to that sort of thing. When Dennis would encounter such a moment, his shoulders would shiver, and his eyes would well up with tears. I knew exactly how he felt.

I remember teaching Morten Lauridsen's *Lux aeterna* to the University Chorus at NEIU in preparation for my last concert there. I started the very first rehearsal with the beginning of the "Agnus Dei," taking time to shape and balance the first phrase as best I could in about ten minutes until the entire chorus felt immersed in the warmth and beauty of that phrase. [3]

Dennis Burmeister

[3] *"Lux aeterna" is a section of the Catholic Missa pro defunctis (Mass for the dead, or Requiem). "Agnus Dei" is part of the Ordinary of the Mass, as well as the Requiem Mass. The first phrase of Lauridsen's setting of the "Agnus Dei" is particularly delectable.*

Then I said, "That's why we sing choral music."

I took a moment to observe the reactions of some in the Chorus—Diane, our alto section leader sighed aloud.

And I looked at Dennis, knowing he understood as a kindred spirit. I believe moments like that were healing for him. I believe it was in those moments that he experienced the release he needed to feel emotionally and spiritually content and at peace.

❧ ❧ ❧

The best leaders find a conduit for enrichment and healing; for me, that conduit is music. The transcendence that often accompanies music-making relieves stress and anxiety and is healing for the soul. That music making is a healing activity isn't so much a lesson I've learned, but one I've always inherently known. It's the reason I became a musician, and it's a lesson that becomes more profound and more clearly focused with every musical experience.

Food for thought

- What is it in your life that provides healing?

- Are there individuals for whom your organization is a source of comfort and solace? Are you then mindful of everyone else?

- What meaningful activities can you introduce to your group to encourage wellness?

♭ Life Is About Tension and Release

I sang with the Grant Park Symphony Chorus in Chicago for about ten years, mostly under the direction of its founder, Thomas Peck. Singing with Tom and the Grant Park Chorus was a wonderful experience, both musically and socially. It was a great way to pass the summer. [1]

[1] The Grant Park Music Festival is a summer concert series featuring the Grant Park Symphony Orchestra and Chorus. It was begun in 1931 by Mayor Anton Cermak to boost the morale of Chicago residents during the Great Depression. It claims to be the only free, outdoor, classical music series in the country.

Tom was very short and rotund with thinning hair and a beard, which he often stroked while pontificating. He spoke in a way that was meant to demonstrate healthy vocalism, which is to say he used excessive naso-pharyngeal resonance[2] (imagine speaking with a very open throat and feeling your voice in your sinuses)—something many of his chorus singers imitated good-naturedly when we spoke to one another.

Tom often used the podium as a pulpit, which seemed inappropriate to me, even if I usually agreed with what he had to say. He was also very plain-spoken about pretty much everything and often said outrageous things, whether intentionally or not.

Once he was asked to prepare a smaller choir for what was termed the "Midwest première" of Andrew Lloyd Webber's *Requiem*,[3] and I was invited to sing in that group. At our one and only room rehearsal, it was easy to see Tom had a certain disdain for the musical style of the composition, and, to make his point, he led the choir through a particularly sentimental passage.

After we had sung it, he remarked, "Now doesn't that just make your sphincter pucker?"

A year before he died, Tom was giving away some of his books and music and selling some of it, with the proceeds being donated to an AIDS clinic. It was during that summer that I began to understand tension and release. Tom made reference to it in musical terms several times that summer.

But in one poignant moment, while rehearsing a particularly dramatic section of music, he stopped to again ask that we, the Chorus, understand the importance of establishing tension and release.

And then he said, "It's the sweet release we feel after a climactic moment in a phrase or section of music. And it's the sweetest release we'll know until that great final release."

There was a pause before the rehearsal continued, and we all wondered about his foreboding comment.

The following summer at a Chorus rehearsal, we were informed that Tom died at his home in St. Louis at the age of 56. The cause of death was AIDS, according to a spokesperson for the St. Louis Symphony Orchestra.

Michael Cullen, his long-time accompanist, was asked to prepare the Chorus to sing a couple of motets at a Grant Park concert in Tom's memory. I remember rehearsing "O vos omnes" by the most famous Spanish composer of the 16th century, Tomás Luis de Victoria.[4] Michael commented that musical composition might just as well have ceased at the end of the Renaissance—

---

[2] *The nasopharynx is the area behind the soft palate leading from the pharynx (basically the back of the throat) to the nasal passages. You know it as the place where you feel post-nasal drip during a cold or allergy attack. It's an important resonator for singers, used to help properly "place" the voice.*

[3] *Andrew Lloyd Webber has enjoyed enormous success as a musical theater composer (Evita, Cats, Phantom of the Opera, Sunset Boulevard—the list is long). The most popular movement from his Requiem, "Pie Jesu," has been performed and recorded by numerous artists.*

[4] *"O vos omnes" was often set by Renaissance composers for the Tenebrae Responsories for Holy Saturday (the day before Easter Sunday). Victoria's setting is one of the most famous. The translation of the text is:*
O all ye that pass by the way, attend and see:
If there be any sorrow like to my sorrow.
Attend, all ye people, and see my sorrow:
If there be any sorrow like to my sorrow.

Inspiring Harmony

Petrillo Music Shell, Chicago

Thomas Peck

it had reached a stylistic pinnacle.

When we performed the motet at the Petrillo Music Shell in Grant Park, it was a still summer night, and we sang with an empty podium and a conductor's stand with the music on it.

Shortly after the performance started, a bird began to fly just over the heads of the audience, warbling loudly enough to be heard by the singers. It's the only time I can remember hearing a bird so close to the stage. As we neared the end of the piece, a gentle breeze blew, literally turning the page on the conductor's music. I felt then, as we found musical release at the end of the motet, that Tom had finally experienced "that great final release."

Life so often seems a struggle: for success, for money, for happiness. Doesn't it make more sense to accept the reality that life ebbs and flows, and we're better off embracing it than fighting it? I think there is a certain rhythm inherent in the universe and in each of our lives—some moments are tense, anticipating the release that is coming, and some offer repose. From the micro-rhythms of our daily routines, meals with friends, and work, to the macro-rhythms of career, life-long family relationships, and aging, we are inextricably bound to the rhythm of life. To resist it is to be perpetually off balance, struggling, and discontented. To "go with the flow" and accept the inevitable ups and downs allows us to be more in sync with life and more able to be content, no matter our present state.

As leaders, we are expected to guide others toward certain goals, but we must be willing to accept the inevitable corporate rhythm that evolves within groups. That sometimes requires relinquishing control—a difficult challenge for many of us. Inspiring harmony sometimes means allowing for tension and release to naturally occur, lest we inspire disharmony by our inflexibility.

When we embrace tension and release, we become better at our jobs, our relationships, and our art. We are in tune with the rhythm of life until we, too, experience "that great final release."

Food for thought

- What is the natural rhythm of your group? What are the main influences on that rhythm?

- What influence do you have over it? Are you willing to relinquish some degree of control in the interest of harmony when energy is ebbing? Can you sense when your group is receptive to a nudge to get some positive energy flowing again?

ⓗ Be A Servant

I spent twelve years singing High Holidays services in three different synagogues. I'm not Jewish, but I played the part for eleven of those twelve years. (One year was with a Reform congregation, and they couldn't have cared less if the singers were Jewish.) My first experience, though, was in an Orthodox congregation—talk about baptism by fire!

As the choir gathered before *S'lichot*,[1] the rabbi came to inspect the troops. Replete with a long gray beard, tall black hat, and floor-length black robe, he strolled past the choir, stopped to look at me, and said with a heavy Eastern European accent, "I see we have a new member in the choir."

"Yes, Rabbi," I replied.

"And what is your name?" he queried.

"It's Michael," I answered cautiously.

"I did not hear you," he said.

"Mi-cha-el," I said, as it is pronounced in Hebrew.

He pressed further, "And what does this mean?"

"Like unto God," I replied bravely (I had fortunately learned that from my parents).

> [1] S'lichot (also spelled "Selichot") are communal prayers for divine forgiveness. The first night of S'lichot (in the Ashkenazic tradition), when the choir would sing, is the Saturday before Rosh Hashanah. It is a service of penitential poems and prayers in preparation for the High Holidays.

The Rabbi smiled and said, "Welcome to the *shul*,[2] Mi-cha-el."

Two years later I began a ten-year relationship with A.G. Beth Israel Congregation in Lincolnwood, Illinois.[3] When I was called to be a singer for the Holidays, no one mentioned the singers were expected to be Jewish.

So when I arrived at the first rehearsal, the first order of business was to figure out how we singers would answer the question of our lineage. (The "choir" was actually a men's quartet, and I think the only Jewish person among us was the *chazzan*.[4]) We learned the basics about what to say and not say if approached by members of the congregation, and over the years, I learned a lot of standard greetings and phrases.

Still, I felt badly about deceiving people regarding my true identity.

But as time passed, I was asked to play piano for a few Sisterhood lunches, provide a band for an annual dinner dance (complete with vocal performances by three great guys from the congregation known as "The Granddads"), and when a new *chazzan* came to A.G., I was asked to be the music director for the choir—to essentially help lead the quartet during rehearsals and services. It even got to the point that when a new singer joined the quartet, members of the congregation would come to me privately to ask if I knew whether the new member was Jewish. I suppose I was the one they had come to trust.

One memorable *Rosh Hashanah* morning, the cantor, Dov, overslept and was late to the synagogue. He was very overweight and in poor health, but he still had to walk to *shul* because of the holiday.

When 9:15 rolled around, Rabbi Irving Glickman came off the *bimah* [5] to let the choir know he was ready to begin the *Torah* service.[6]

I told him the choir was ready, but we had no cantor.

He simply said, "It's time, let's begin."

[2] Shul *is a Yiddish word (derived from German) literally meaning "school." It is used, particularly by Orthodox Jews, to mean the synagogue, emphasizing its purpose as a place of study.*

[3] A.G. *stands for "Austro-Galician."*

[4] Chazzan *(also spelled "Hazzan") is the cantor who leads the congregation in prayer. The Chazzan is expected to be well versed in Jewish religious education, as well as musically and vocally trained.*

Rabbi Irving Glickman

Inspiring Harmony

> [5] *The* bimah *(also spelled "bema") is the raised platform from which services are led and the Torah is read. The choir was positioned front and center on the* bimah.

> [6] *Before the Torah is read, the Torah scrolls are removed from a cabinet on the* bimah *called the* Aron Kodesh *("holy ark") and carried throughout the congregation. The choir sang until the scrolls were returned.*

"But we can't start without the *chazzan*," I protested.

"We have to start; it's time," he answered. "You do it. You've been here long enough to know the prayers."

"I know the choral responses," I objected, "but I don't know all the prayers."

"Well, let's go," he said. "We have to start now."

So we all walked onto the *bimah*, I smiled at the *Rebbitzen* (the Rabbi's wife), as usual, looked at the Rabbi who gave me a nod, then turned to the congregation and belted out "*Sh'ma Yisrael ...*"[7]

Fortunately, the cantor made it to the *bimah* by the time the *Torah* had made its way around the congregation. We were all pretty sure he had a mild heart attack that morning trying to hurry to the synagogue. His face was pale and yellowish when he arrived, and he kept gripping his chest, unable to get enough oxygen.

In fact, he passed away from a major heart attack only a short time later.

> [7] *The Sh'ma (also spelled "Shema") is the oldest daily prayer in Judaism. The first line is translated: "Hear, Israel, the Lord is our G-d; the Lord is One."*

Rabbi Glickman has also passed away since then—he was a good man.

Near the end of my time at A.G., I had a conversation with one of the Granddads, Marvin Rosett, who came to me often for voice lessons and was the only person I was aware of who knew I wasn't Jewish. I told him I had been feeling badly for some time about deceiving the congregation about my faith and was thinking of leaving the synagogue because of it.

He proceeded to describe to me at some length how meaningful my service to the congregation had been and how the music we all made had contributed to their worship.

In that moment, I realized that I had, indeed, been a servant, and that my service impacted other people in an important way. I stayed for two more years of High Holidays at A.G. and sang in many other synagogues in the Chicago area along the way.

I've watched people shed a tear as I sang the *Yizkor* prayer on *Yom Kippur*.[8] I've watched people kneel before a statue of the Virgin Mary as I sang "*Ave Maria.*"[9] I've watched people with their eyes closed in fervent prayer raise their hands to God as I sang a favorite gospel song. I've watched military veterans stand proudly at attention, saluting the flag as I sang our National Anthem. I've watched people joyously sing along with a favorite Christmas carol, folk song, or drinking song.

In all cases, the music, the texts, the experiences were deeply moving and meaningful and so important in the lives of those people. And my role in each case was to serve. To understand that has brought me a great sense of satisfaction and fulfillment.

> [8] *The* Yizkor *prayer is a memorial prayer for the departed. It is recited or sung four times a year, including on Yom Kippur (the "Day of Atonement," the holiest day of the year).*

> [9] *"Ave Maria" is a traditional Catholic intercessory prayer to the Virgin Mary, the mother of Jesus.*

Great leaders are servants at heart, always looking out for the best interests of others. They put self-interest aside in service to the well-being of the community. To lead with grace is to serve—there is no higher calling than to serve others. It is the essence of being human and an essential part of leadership.

Food for thought:

- Are you a servant leader? Why do you think so?

- Do you see yourself more as a director than as part of the team? How do you think your group sees you?

- What could you do differently to ensure your words and actions are always in furtherance of the best interest of your group?

Who Gets the Credit? Or the Blame?

We've all heard "it's more blessed to give than to receive," but how important is it to get credit for giving? A true sign of spiritual growth is to be able to sacrifice something for another's benefit without expecting anything in return.

I learned about *mitzvah* from Irving Glickman, the Rabbi of whom I spoke in the previous chapter. He was teaching the congregation during the Holidays one year, and he described the different levels of *mitzvah* (literally meaning precept or commandment), in reference to Maimonides' "Eight Levels of Charity."[1]

[1] Maimonides (Moses ben Maimon, also known as "Rambam") was a 12th-century Sephardic scholar and philosopher, who described "Eight Levels of Charity."

The second highest level, he said, is to give to the poor without knowing to whom the gift is given, and without the recipient knowing from whom it was received. This is performing a *mitzvah* "solely for the sake of heaven."

How often life seems to come with a scorecard. "I owe you one" implies that, in order to keep everything fair and equitable, a favor must be returned with a favor of more or less equal value. Sometimes it's more difficult to be a gracious recipient of a gift than to be a gracious giver. But our human nature seems to pull most strongly toward wanting recognition for having made a sacrificial gift to another.

Even more challenging is to be willing to share the blame for something that was largely or entirely someone else's fault. The urge to defend oneself can be very strong, especially when there is something of value at stake. While no one wants to be a patsy, there are times when taking or at least sharing the blame is prudent and even necessary.

While an undergraduate student at the University of Iowa, I worked one summer in a cornfield driving a de-tasseling machine while high school students rode along in "buckets" pulling tassels.[2] The crew foreman had told me that because it was such a hot summer, we could sit at one end of the field to rest, as long as the owner didn't see us.

Sure enough, as we sat there one day, the owner came along and chewed me out for sitting down on the job.

Rather than accepting the blame, I threw the crew foreman under the bus and told the boss he was the one who told me it was OK. Well, the crew foreman was none too happy about that, as one would expect, and the rest of the summer with him was no fun. I guess it was more important for me to save face and defend myself than to preserve my relationship with the crew foreman—a poor choice as it turned out.

> [2] Removing corn tassels from one variety of plant allows it to be fertilized by the tassels of another variety, thereby producing a hybrid.

I think this is one of the most difficult aspects of becoming a mature human being. Image is so important, and what others think of us so highly valued, we covet the approval and admiration of those around us. To be blamed for something for which we're not responsible is a hard pill to swallow, but sometimes necessary to maintain good relationships and even to hold on to one's job. To be largely responsible for a good deed or a successful outcome and not be recognized for it is almost as frustrating. But the mature response to such things is to be happy that another person's lot in life has been improved.

~ ~ ~

In the end, who gets the credit or the blame is irrelevant—grace tells us we shouldn't care. As a leader, if you are consistently looking out for the best interests of others, people will often notice, and maybe even follow your example. Sometimes you get the credit, other times maybe not. Sometimes you'll have to take the blame for something you didn't do, but usually you won't. In any case, learning to be content with simply doing the right thing, no matter who gets the credit or the blame, is a major step toward becoming a spiritually whole human being and a successful leader.

Inspiring Harmony

Food for thought:

- When was the last time you felt happiness, simply because someone else's life was improved?

- If your team is successful in reaching a goal, are you quick to share the credit and praise with others?

- If your team fails in its efforts and the blame falls on you, are you willing to say "the buck stops here?" Can you inspire your team to redouble its efforts to succeed the next time?

Michael Melton

First, Land the Airplane

And now, for a complete change of pace …

I've worked as a part-time Certified Flight Instructor (CFI) since 1990. Along the way, I added an Instrument Rating and Multi-Engine Rating to my teaching certificate, allowing me to train pilots to fly solely by reference to instruments (in the clouds) and in airplanes with more than one engine. But first, I had to become a Private Pilot myself, then add an Instrument Rating to my Private Pilot certificate, then earn a Commercial Pilot certificate. It was during my instrument training that I learned to "first, land the airplane."

I did my private and instrument training at Midway Airport in Chicago, once the busiest airport in the world. Now dwarfed by many larger airports, it's only one mile square. Flight training was done mostly south of the airport since Chicago was mostly north, so

Mike with a Piper Seminole

Inspiring Harmony

Navigation instruments highlighted

the Gary, Indiana, airport was a good place to conduct practice instrument approaches. In these sessions pilots learn to approach the runway without outside visual references—solely by using the instruments on the panel.

My instrument flight instructor, Kevin, was a good pilot, but not a good teacher. I did learn a valuable lesson from him, however, in rather dramatic fashion.

Kevin and I took off from Midway Airport for the short flight to Gary Airport to shoot practice approaches. We contacted Chicago Approach Control to request a practice approach to Runway 30 at Gary. After some necessary maneuvering, we were handed off to Gary's control tower to complete the approach. Everything seemed to be going well …

As you might imagine, there are many steps to completing an instrument approach. On an Instrument Landing System [1] approach (ILS—the type we were flying), one of the secondary steps is to time the approach from a specified point. Timing an ILS is good practice, but not the most important piece of the puzzle.

About halfway down the final approach course I realized I had forgotten to start the timer, and I groused to Kevin about my blunder.

"Just pay attention," he scolded.

> [1] An Instrument Landing System (ILS) approach is called a "precision approach" because it provides both vertical and lateral guidance to the runway. Indicators on the instrument panel (usually "needles") show the pilot if a turn is needed to stay on the "localizer" (lateral guidance), or if a climb or descent is needed to stay on the "glide slope" (vertical guidance).

80

Michael Melton

This so-called "precision approach" became quite imprecise after that. While beating myself up about forgetting to time the approach, I let myself get too high and right of course—and flew right past the airport. I was wearing foggles,[2] a view-limiting device that blocked my view of the outside world, and I became disoriented.

Now, if you know Gary and its airport, you know that due north of the town sits Lake Michigan, and Runway 30 points northwest, so too high and off course to the right was a bad place to be. When Kevin decided he had let this go far enough, he asked me to remove my foggles and take a look.

Sure enough, we were descending into Lake Michigan. That seemed a bad way to end this approach, so we climbed away on the missed approach,[3] and I proceeded to kick myself for being so stupid.

"It's all about prioritizing," Kevin said. "First, land the airplane—then think about what you can do better the next time."

[2] *Pilots training for the Instrument Rating wear a view-limiting device intended to block the pilot's view of everything except the instrument panel. There are a few different types of these devices—the one I was wearing is called "foggles."*

[3] *The "missed approach" is the part of the approach procedure that is flown if a landing cannot be completed, usually because of inadequate ceiling or visibility (or in my case, because the pilot is too far off course).*

I've shared those words of wisdom with my students many times. The phrase certainly rings true for performers, but it's also true for leaders. When we fixate on one mistake, rather than looking ahead to what's coming next, the mistakes compound and can result in disaster. Mistakes will happen—it's inevitable.

Vladimir Horowitz

> [4] *Mistakes in recorded performance, including studio recordings, were more common in past decades than they are now. While this illustrative story about Horowitz is often repeated (I cannot attest to its veracity), the reality is that many of his (and others' of his generation) recordings include mistakes.*

There's a story of the great pianist, Vladimir Horowitz, making a recording of Chopin. After one particular take, the producer pointed out there was a wrong note in the performance.

Horowitz said "I know, that's OK."

When the producer pressed him to play it again to try to eliminate the mistake, Horowitz replied, "That's as musically as I can play it—the wrong note will have to stay."

For him, the musicality of the performance was more important than "perfection." [4]

※ ※ ※

We worry so much about mistakes that success, satisfaction, and happiness can all be compromised. Perhaps it's the knowledge that we are being critiqued or judged by others, particularly by those who may have some authority over us. Or perhaps, as is the case with me, it's just a little too much perfectionism. As leaders, our mistakes will often be on display, and fixating on them can be an easy trap, especially if we're hearing negative criticism. After many years of frustration, my advice is: Always strive to be better, but learn to be content with where you are right now. And whatever blunders you may make along the way, "first, land the airplane."

Food for thought:

- Can you remember a time when one simple mistake led to others, resulting in some type of failure? How did you "land your plane?" Or did you crash?

- Are you a perfectionist or overly concerned about what others will think if you make mistakes or allow them to pass uncorrected?

- As a leader, are you able to overlook the mistakes of others in the interest of the long-term success of your group?

Michael Melton

ⓗ Failure Is Absolutely an Option

I've jumped out of a perfectly good airplane twice in my life. It's something I always wanted to try, and when I was in my 20s, my brother, Myron, and I decided to go to a small rural airport in Kansas to give it a go.

After signing the usual waivers (you know, the kind that says you're responsible for anything that happens, and they're responsible for nothing—"you could die doing this; please sign here"), we spent the day training for our first and only jump. It began as an exciting day for both of us.

You may have heard the saying, "If at first you don't succeed, skydiving is not for you."

Well, I guess I wasn't paying attention because I had an emergency that afternoon as I left the airplane.

It was a static line jump, meaning the ripcord was attached

Mike with his brother, Myron

to a hook inside the plane, just in case the skydiver had trouble pulling the cord for any reason. I made the mistake of not going "spread eagle" immediately upon exiting the plane, caught some wind on my upper body, and ended up head down.

Then, as the static line pulled my ripcord, the lines attached to the parachute wrapped around one of my legs. I managed to pull my body into a tuck and unwrap the lines, allowing myself to fall feet first, but at least one of the lines had looped over the chute creating what is known as a "Mae West."[1]

That often causes the chute to spin (when "Mae" is lopsided), which mine did, with the risers (the straps through which the lines are channeled) then wrapping around my neck. After freeing my head and realizing I had a bad chute, the next step was to deploy an emergency chute.

Unfortunately, we were using old Army-style chutes in which the emergency chute was not spring loaded, so I had to release and pull the emergency chute from its pack, and then throw it out to the side.

Mike in a jump suit

The emergency chute didn't take air at first, so the next task was to "buggy whip" the lines on the emergency chute to get it to take air.

> [1] *The "Mae West" is a type of round parachute malfunction that causes the canopy to be divided into large lobes, and was consequently named after the generously proportioned late actress, Mae West. Once a "Mae West" has formed, it's virtually impossible for the chute to fully open.*

When it did, my near free fall was instantly slowed to about 15 mph—quite a jolt, especially with the pack strapped on between my legs. I was feeling lucky to have an emergency chute inflated and the spinning stopped so the two chutes didn't become intertwined, making them both useless.

When I was finally able to look down, I was horrified to see a road directly below me. *Perfect*, I thought. *I'll save my neck in the air only to land on a road and get hit by a truck.*

Those old, round Army chutes aren't steerable either, by the way, so I pulled a little on a couple of the emergency chute's lines—not enough to collapse the chute, but enough to get a little drift and land in a soybean field about twenty feet from the road.

The instructor, seeing what happened, jumped right after me and guided his much superior rectangular chute to a landing right next to me.

"Great emergency procedure," he said after checking that I was OK. "You'll be great the next time out."

Next time my ass. You won't get me to do this again!

When I asked how close I had come to disaster, he told me I was within 1,000 feet and about ten seconds from hitting the ground when the emergency chute inflated. I hitched a ride back to the airport, got on the back of my brother's motorcycle (of all things), and couldn't wait to get back home.

A few days later, as I thought about what had happened, I had a gnawing feeling that I just couldn't leave it at that. Even though I had handled the emergency well enough, it was still my fault the chute failed, and I just couldn't live with that.

"Mae West" parachute malfunction

So, upon returning to Chicago, I found a skydiving school in Hinckley, Illinois, and called them to schedule a little remedial training and another jump. Other than a moment just before jumping when my rational mind questioned the lunacy of my actions, everything went smoothly, and I felt satisfied and happy that I had "gotten back on the horse."

I haven't felt the desire to jump out of an airplane since.

The failure that was much harder for me to overcome was in my senior year of college. I had double-majored in voice and piano, so I gave two recitals as a senior. My piano recital had gone very well, but I chose a very ambitious program for my voice recital. Now, as a voice teacher, I can look back and wonder why my teacher allowed me to take on repertoire that was clearly beyond my vocal ability. But I suppose I had persuaded him I could handle it, and I remember thinking at the time I could do just about anything.

I was also working at a service station that year, during one of the coldest winters in Iowa history (1978-79). The combination of breathing extremely cold air and pushing my voice beyond its limits proved to be too much at the recital. After singing the first half well, I faltered during the Vaughan Williams "Four Hymns for Tenor, Viola, and Piano." [2]

I turned to the other two musicians after the second hymn and opted to cut the third.

After singing the last one, I left the stage, and my teacher came back to see how I was doing. I could barely speak, let alone sing, so we chose to end the recital before the last set. He had to announce to a full recital hall that I was indisposed and unable to complete the recital, and I had to take a final bow before trying to keep a smile on while receiving condolences from the audience members who were kind enough to come backstage to see me.

> [2] Vaughan Williams' "Four Hymns" is a beautiful but vocally challenging set of pieces. They require a more mature, developed voice than I possessed as a senior in college, and they proved to be my undoing at my senior recital.

It was a few years before I could sing again with confidence, without feeling terrified I might lose my voice and embarrass myself again. I continued to sing, however, learned from my experience, and have since enjoyed many years of singing and teaching singers.

What a loss it would have been in my life had I chosen to stop singing.

❧ ❧ ❧

We have all heard stories about people who have failed, only to later have some tremendous success. Thomas Edison once said, "I have not failed. I've just found 10,000 ways that won't work." He also said, "Our greatest weakness lies in giving up. The most certain way to succeed is always to try just one more time."

Becoming a leader for the first time can be terrifying for many people, and the fear of failure can be overwhelming. Just remember, you are in a leadership position because others think you should be, you're excited about the work, or you are at least willing to take on an important challenge. If you happen to meet with some failure along the way, you can always regroup and try again.

Success often requires perseverance, fortitude, patience, hard work, and usually a bit of luck. And for many successful people, failure comes before success. The tragedy comes when we give in to failure and stop trying.

Food for thought:

- Have you given up on a dream, simply because you have experienced failure? Are you not taking on a leadership role for fear of failure?

- Every organization will experience some degree of failure at some point along the way. As a leader, how should you acknowledge that, learn from it, and inspire your group to move forward?

- Is your team willing to stretch, try new ideas, and risk failure in order to grow?

Coping with Tragedy

An inevitable part of the human experience is tragedy: events that are sad, frightening, depressing, or horrific happen to us all sooner or later. How we deal with them can mean the difference between optimism and pessimism, hopefulness and despair. How we deal with them as leaders can make all the difference in how others face tragedy and process its sometimes devastating consequences. It is a sobering responsibility.

I've known four colleagues who have been murdered, all of them singers in Chicago.[1] The first was found in his kitchen with a knife in his back; the second was stabbed to death in his bed; the third was strangled in an apparent sexual encounter gone awry, so it wasn't known whether it was murder or accidental death; and the fourth was beaten and thrown into the Chicago River, apparently because of drug money he owed.

> [1] This is an improbable distinction to be sure, and one I would be happy not to own.

Communities of people usually come together to mourn such losses, and musicians seem particularly good at it. We'll gather together to share memories and to eulogize the person we've lost, but the focal point of the remembrance is often music—either a performance by a few for the benefit of the others or group singing.

I find it difficult to sing at times like that, but making music, singing in particular, is very healing. One reason for that phenomenon is that music is a unique language. When words alone don't seem enough, hearing them set to music can deliver them in a different and more powerful way. And when words fail us altogether, music speaks to us in its own language, a language we cannot adequately describe with our words, but one we all understand. It somehow facilitates our communal grieving of a loss.

It is incumbent on leaders to provide guidance, consolation, and a means for grieving to the people we are leading. To tell others how they should grieve is not always helpful, but to provide a context for grieving and means of comfort is critically important.

September 11, 2001, was a Tuesday, which meant I would be flight instructing in the morning and conducting a University Chorus rehearsal at Northeastern Illinois University in the evening. At Chicago Executive Airport (then Palwaukee Airport) that morning, everyone was glued to a television watching the terrible events unfold. It wasn't long before our nation's airspace was closed, so no flight instruction would take place that day—not that I could or would have flown, anyway.

I knew that evening's rehearsal could not be "business as usual" either, so I considered how to help the Chorus process the events of the day. Rather than leading a warmup and launching into our music, I told the Chorus I thought we should first talk about what had happened that morning.

As one would expect, comments ranged from head-scratching questions, to anger, to attempts at an explanation. I tried to acknowledge each person's thoughts and feelings respectfully, but I thought it best not to leave the conversation open ended.

Leonard Bernstein

As it seemed time to wrap things up, I read a passage from Leonard Bernstein's "Tribute to John F. Kennedy," his "reply to violence" written three days after the assassination of President Kennedy.

Bernstein said, "We musicians, like everyone else, are numb with sorrow at this murder, and with rage at the senselessness of the crime. But this sorrow and rage will not inflame us to seek retribution; rather they will inflame our art. Our music will never again be quite the same. This will be our reply to violence: to make music more intensely, more beautifully, more devotedly than ever before."

I added that I concurred with Bernstein and that I believed our best response to such violence was to create beauty—to make music.

Then we took an early break so everyone could walk around a bit, have some water, and talk with each other.

Inspiring Harmony

After the break, we began the rehearsal as we normally would have and spent the rest of the evening singing.

Every individual and every group will process tragedy differently, but there are certain things that are universal:

- Everyone's thoughts and feelings are valid.
- Everyone needs an opportunity to grieve—ignoring a tragedy does not allow for healing.
- One of the most healing activities for humans, especially in times of tragedy, is to create something beautiful.

Creating something beautiful can take many forms, of course, but for me, it's making music.

One other point about being a leader: To whatever extent necessary, you must put your own grief on hold while facilitating the grieving process for your group.

Mike's father, Merle

I remember watching my father, a Christian minister, lead countless funerals and memorial services, often for family members and close friends. He always offered words of comfort to those gathered, but rarely cried or showed much overt emotion while conducting the service.

When I was a young adult, I asked him how he managed to do that, and he said, "I have to put my own feelings aside temporarily. I can't minister to others if I'm the one who is overcome with emotion. I have to save my crying for later."

❦ ❦ ❦

Not every day is a 9/11, but every person with whom you work as a leader will come to your group at some point having suffered some sort of hurt. It could be as minor as a little misunderstanding at work or as devastating as the loss of a loved one.

Remember to ask yourself on any given day, as you look upon the people you lead, "How many of these individuals are struggling today with some type of problem, however large or small? Are they coping with some tragedy, and how can I help them?"

In this simple act of awareness, kindness, and grace, you'll find yourself a more empathetic leader.

Food for thought:

- How have you coped with tragedy in your own life? In the lives of others?
- As a leader, how have you or would you respond to a tragic event impacting your group? Consider how you would allow for and even facilitate grieving—then find an appropriate, respectful way to move on.

ⓗ To Worry or Not to Worry

… That is the question.

For the longest time I declared I was not a worrier, but over the years I've come to accept the fact that I am. I know it's pointless. I know it causes unhealthy stress. I know it hinders my ability to be productive. But much of the time I can't seem to curb it, so this is definitely a lesson with which I am continuing to struggle.

Like so many of our natural impulses, worrying defies reason. Much as telling someone how safe it is to fly doesn't allay his or her fear of flying, telling someone to "just don't worry" is equally pointless. I think learning to cope with the tendency to worry about things, especially things out of our control, only comes from mindful experience.

With every worrisome experience I have, I remind myself, "You can worry about this, and it will all work out somehow. Or you can not worry about this, and it will still work out somehow." Worry certainly doesn't help bring about a good solution; if anything, it hinders it.

When I was hired at Northeastern Illinois University (NEIU) in 1996 to teach voice, I was also invited to conduct the University Chorus, the only choir at NEIU at the time. My predecessor, James Lucas, had coincidentally been a doctoral student at the University of Iowa while I was an undergrad there in the late 1970s. Jim was a

James Lucas

very good conductor, but he had had enough of conducting, and the Music Department was struggling at that time, so he decided to tackle other challenges there.

When I picked up my first University Chorus class list and went to the first rehearsal that fall, I realized I had only nine singers to work with—eight women and one man—and two of the women couldn't match pitch.[1]

Talk about reason to worry! How would I ever put together a viable concert with that group?

Rather than throwing up my hands in defeat, however, I decided to do some recruiting and find a way to make it work.

Within a few weeks, I had sixteen women in the ensemble, but still only one man, who really wanted to be there. I also had a very limited budget, and the concert had already been scheduled for Wednesday, the night before Thanksgiving.

So, the first thing I did was promise the singers a party if they would commit to being in the Chorus and performing that Wednesday evening.

> [1] Some refer to the apparent inability to match pitch as being "tone deaf." Barring an auditory or vocal problem, I believe anyone can be taught to sing in tune, but some people do have more innate pitch sensitivity than others. For those who have difficulty, the problem is usually a matter of coordination. They may hear the pitch correctly, but have difficulty producing the same pitch (frequency) with their voices. This issue is also addressed in the chapter titled "You're Never Too Old."

Then came the matter of repertoire. I knew of a piece called *Mass to St. Anthony* by Lou Harrison for unison voices, trumpet, harp, and strings. Good instrumentalists can complete an otherwise thin sound as long as the balance is good—so I called on some old friends to come and help us out. Then I announced that NEIU now had a women's ensemble and programmed some beautiful standard works for women's choir and piano, placing the two women with vocal problems nearest the piano for some pitch support.

Still the one man, a bass, needed something more to sing, so I asked two of the stronger women in the group to sing soprano and alto, while I sang tenor in J.S. Bach's motet *Lobet den Herrn*.

The concert actually came off reasonably well, and I was relieved to have it behind me. The Music Department steadily improved in the following years, and the choral program grew with it. But no matter how much the choirs improved, I never really stopped worrying about it.

Inspiring Harmony

The point is, I would have done whatever I needed to do to make that first concert a success, no matter what. And it's possible it could have been a failure, despite my best efforts. But worrying about it certainly didn't help. I did fret about the details—I always do—and I did lose sleep that semester, but I'm convinced that fretting did nothing more than make me tired for the concert.

After sixteen years as Director of Choral Activities at NEIU, we managed to grow two healthy choirs and, with the help of other area choirs and a larger budget, performed such masterworks as the Brahms and Mozart *Requiems*, Vaughan Williams' *Five Mystical Songs*, and Lauridsen's *Lux Aeterna*, all with full orchestra.

Northeastern Illinois University and North Park University
Brahms, Ein deutsches Requiem
Michael Melton, conductor
Marlene Meier, soprano   Bradley Whaley, baritone
April 21, 2009   NEIU Auditorium

I think that would have happened with or without all the worry.

༺ ༺ ༺

So, to worry or not to worry … why bother?

It clouds your thinking, impedes your progress, and adds unhealthy stress to your life. As a leader, it can create or exacerbate apprehension within your group and cause others to feel less comfortable and confident in your leadership. The lesson learned is: just don't worry.

But, if you can figure out how saying "just don't worry" makes it all go away, please let me know.

Food for thought:

- How much time and energy do you waste worrying about things beyond your control?

- Was there a time when you felt anxious as a leader and your team became anxious, as well? Did you have coping mechanisms to put yourself and them at ease?

- When you begin to feel apprehension creeping in, are you able to take a step back? Can you see the big picture, make a plan, and know that, worry or not, things will work out?

The Whole Truth?

"The whole truth and nothing but the truth …"

"Honesty is the best policy …"

"I cannot tell a lie …"

For most of us, the idea of always being honest is ingrained from childhood. Being completely honest is moral, righteous, and noble, and to be dishonest is shameful. But, as with most things in life, honesty isn't quite so black or white; dare I say there are shades of honesty.

And there are times when complete honesty can do more harm than good.

As I described in the previous chapter, the first several years of my tenure as Director of Choral Activities at Northeastern Illinois University (NEIU) were rebuilding years for the choral program and the Music Department in general. I did a lot of recruiting, both from the university student body and from the broader community. The membership of the choirs was growing, and the level of musical performance was improving, albeit slowly. I couldn't afford to be too picky about qualifications for membership, especially in the University Chorus, so my only requirements were that singers be able to sing in tune with reasonably good tone. Of course, that allowed for quite a range of musical abilities within any given section of the Chorus.

Conducting rehearsals in a way that was not too challenging for the weakest singer and not too boring for the strongest singer became quite the balancing act.

It seems in almost every group of humans, there is at least one person who feels very strongly about how things should be done. They seem to become committee chairs, board presidents, etc., because they really need to make sure things get done just the way they think they should.

And, I've found, diplomacy isn't always their strong suit.

I had one such singer in the bass section of the Chorus during those early years at NEIU. John (not his real name) had sung with a few amateur choirs in Chicago, and he joined a fairly weak bass section in the Chorus. He seemed frustrated from time to time with his section, but he crossed the line when he decided to telephone me to criticize my conducting.

Actually, there were a few phone calls, ostensibly to offer suggestions for improving the Chorus. I've always been open to comments and suggestions, but his became gradually more pointed and, at first, critical of his fellow basses.

I answered his concerns by saying they had all come with differing levels of experience and ability, and we should simply work together to be as good as possible.

My explanations didn't seem to satisfy him, as he continued to call, until one day he called particularly upset to say, "I think the reason you aren't doing anything to correct the bass section problems is because you can't hear the problems."

Critical listening, of course, is one of the most fundamental skills of a conductor, so his comment didn't sit well with me.

After a little back and forth, him attacking and me explaining (defending), I said, "Please don't call me again—and perhaps you would be happier singing in another choir."

He apparently agreed because he left the Chorus soon after.

An important skill for conductors, but also for leaders of any group, is using appropriate filters. The filtering questions you use in your situation may be different from mine, but as examples, here are the ones I continually ask myself when conducting a choir or orchestra:

- "Which of the problems I hear are most urgent?"

- "How many corrections can this ensemble absorb at one time, and how many of those will stick?"

- "What is the energy of the group at this rehearsal? Do the musicians seem ready to work and improve, or are they lethargic and resisting?"

- "Where are we in the rehearsal process?"
- "How long can certain issues wait for correction?"
- "Am I reinforcing mistakes by not correcting them immediately?"

And then come the two most important questions:

- "Is this choir, orchestra, or section capable of making the improvement I'm hoping for?"
- "If not, will my continuing to push for the improvement become demoralizing?"

Those last two questions were the ones John didn't seem to understand. He wanted me to be brutally honest with the bass section about their shortcomings, but I thought complete honesty would damage their morale and ultimately degrade our performance.

Besides, I needed those basses in my choir, and I didn't see the need to hurt their feelings.

Telling the whole truth isn't always the best approach. I'm not suggesting lying whenever it may be convenient or to avoid having to face a harsh reality that needs facing. But I am saying the consequences of complete honesty can be unnecessarily hurtful to others. I think it behooves us to be circumspect about if and how we share the information we have about others, as well as the opinions we have about them. We should be mindful of nurturing relationships, especially with those we lead. A little encouragement can inspire people to reach for better things, but badgering can lead to a defeatist attitude and failure. And consider these possibilities:

1) in the end, the whole truth may be revealed to the other person by other means,

2) the other person may never know or need to know the whole truth, so what harm has been done, or

3) you may come to realize you were wrong about what you believed about the other person in the first place.

The matter of honesty is one of the grayer areas leaders must face. What's best for one person in a given situation may not be best for another. Choosing the most graceful way forward requires us to be considerate, thoughtful, and compassionate in our words and actions. Find the degree of honesty that makes sense in every situation—it may not be the whole truth.

Food for thought:

- Are you really looking out for the best interests of others when you speak "the truth"? Can you think of situations in the group you lead where saying everything you believe to be true would be more hurtful than helpful?

- Think about those filtering questions I use when conducting a chorus or orchestra. Then create a list of filtering questions appropriate for you and the group you lead.

You Cannot Be Anything You Want to Be

What a disservice we do to young people when we tell them they can be anything they want to be. It simply isn't true.

I encourage people of any age to dream big and imagine all the possibilities that life has to offer. But for leaders and teachers to encourage others to blindly press on toward sometimes nebulous dreams without helping them set realistic goals or assess their strengths and limitations is irresponsible and ultimately hurtful.

In a speech to Chorus America, Garrison Keillor,[1] of "A Prairie Home Companion" fame, waxed eloquent about the joys of group singing. His words were powerful and moving, but one sentence in particular caught my attention: "There comes a time in one's life when you become mature enough to understand that the desire to sing is not the same as having talent."

More than once I've had to have a "come to Jesus" meeting with college students who were, in my opinion, headed down the wrong career path. Whether it was a voice performance major who I knew would never be hired to sing anywhere or a music education major who should never be in front of a classroom, I felt an obligation to gently, but clearly, suggest the student consider another direction.

> [1] *I have been a fan of Garrison Keillor since discovering "A Prairie Home Companion" a few decades ago. I do enjoy his writings and stories, and I love his speech to Chorus America (reprinted in* The Choral Journal, *the monthly publication of the American Choral Directors Association, in December 2000) called "The Power of Choral Singing."*

Michael Melton

I recall a university student who was having a very difficult time dealing emotionally with the pressures of her life. She was a lovely person, but quite unsure of herself, both one-on-one and on stage. During the time she was in my voice studio, she confided in me that she had become so depressed, she was contemplating suicide. She had chosen to be a voice performance major but didn't have the vocal potential or the requisite thick skin to succeed as a professional singer.

Finding a way to guide her away from a singing career (where rejection is a regular occurrence) without shattering her dreams and risking an even deeper spiral into depression was more of a challenge than I wanted. Nevertheless, I brought out the tissues and spent an hour with her one day discussing her strengths, as well as her weaknesses, trying to lead her to the obvious conclusion that she should change majors. (I also referred her to the university's counseling service.)

Garrison Keillor

After a few weeks, she announced with a mixture of resignation and relief that she had decided to change her major to music education. Please don't misunderstand, I absolutely do not believe that "those who can't, teach." [2] Teaching should never be a fallback career. But in this case, she exhibited the potential to be a good teacher. The story has a happy ending: she did become a teacher, and a quite successful one at that.

And I hope she still enjoys singing.

The stories aren't always so dramatic. Years earlier I had a voice student who couldn't for the longest time decide what her goals were, until one day she walked into her lesson to declare she intended to become a "famous chorister"—she would have been the first. There are famous soloists, but no famous choristers that I am aware of.

> [2] *The actual quote from (George) Bernard Shaw's four-act drama,* Man and Superman *("Maxims for Revolutionists") is, "He who can, does; he who cannot, teaches." Woody Allen takes off on the quote in his movie* Annie Hall.

On another occasion, while auditioning singers for the University Chorus, a very nice undergraduate student walked into my office. She was about five feet tall and nearly as big around, with frizzy hair that stood out a foot from her head in all directions. We tried "My Country 'Tis of Thee" in a half-dozen different keys, and she just couldn't sing the notes accurately, no matter what.

As I scratched my head, knowing the news I had to deliver, she said dejectedly, "It wasn't very good, was it."

"No," I said, "I'm afraid it wasn't quite good enough to be able to sing with the Chorus. Do you need this credit to meet a requirement?"

"Yes, I do need one more elective to graduate," she said.

"I'm really sorry about this," I answered. "Do you have any other options?"

Then, with all seriousness, came the funniest reply I've ever heard from a student, "Well, if I can't be in the choir, I guess I'll sign up for basketball."

I really don't think that student was any better equipped for basketball than she was for the Chorus, but I suspect she managed to graduate somehow—she seemed very bright.

❧ ❧ ❧

The lesson learned is: You really cannot be anything you want to be. Leaders have a responsibility to keep that in mind as we guide others. If you're a teacher, a coach, a trainer, or just searching for the right path for yourself, dream big, but temper your enthusiasm with an honest appraisal of your own or someone else's abilities and potential.

Even a graceful dose of reality may hurt at first, but in the long run, you may be avoiding years of frustration and disappointment.

Food for thought:

- Are you being realistic about your own strengths and weaknesses? Is there someone you trust to give you the unvarnished truth?

- If you work with adults pursuing a particular career, is your enthusiastic support of them tempered with a dose of realism? Do you objectively discuss their prospects for success?

- As the team you lead sets the bar ever higher—stretching and taking risks, are you guiding the way by setting goals they can reasonably expect to achieve?

Michael Melton

♮ It Isn't About Perfection

The University Chorus at Northeastern Illinois University was a catchall group of students, faculty, staff, and community residents. We prepared and performed one large work or several smaller works each semester, and the atmosphere in the group was quite familial. Returning community volunteers lent a certain stability to the Chorus, and students rotating in and out every few years ensured a sense of freshness and youth. Although the express purpose of the class was to provide choral music education through study, rehearsal, and performance, students and residents alike understood the experience was about more than just the music.

There were two elderly people in particular for whom singing in the Chorus was especially meaningful. The first was a bass named Bill, whose daughter also sang in the Chorus. Bill was a talker and loved to visit with me during our breaks, regaling me with stories mostly about having played saxophone in a military band.

As Bill aged, his ability to keep up in rehearsal waned, and he required a little extra help to learn the music. He was also in the habit of scooping the pitch at the beginning of most phrases.[1]

After a rehearsal one evening, an undergraduate student came to me to complain about Bill and suggested I ask Bill to leave.

"He's hurting the section and compromising our performance," he said.

[1] *"Scooping the pitch" means to start the note a little too low and then slide up to the correct pitch. This is done frequently in many popular styles of music, but it's stylistically inappropriate when singing "classical" music.*

Inspiring Harmony

Well, first of all, we weren't the Chicago Symphony Chorus—it wasn't as if there was a recording contract out there waiting for us.

And second, Bill would have been devastated had I asked him to leave. The student was indignant when I refused to consider his request and threatened to leave himself. I told him I hoped he would stay and perhaps help Bill (the student was actually a pretty good singer), but Bill would be a part of the Chorus for as long as he wished.

Bill did finally take himself out of the Chorus when he was no longer able to make it to rehearsals, but he continued to attend concerts and always talked about how much it meant to him to have sung with us.[2]

Bill the bass

[2] *Bill's daughter shared with me tearfully one evening how happy she was that Bill was able to sing in the Chorus for several years. It meant as much to her as it did to him.*

The second, even more colorful, Chorus singer was Sophie. Sophie was around eighty years old when she came to the Chorus and wanted me to know about all her past musical experience, including playing the piano. She was still physically active and wanted to be involved in as many activities as possible. She was a self-proclaimed "Atheist Jew" and had a meek little voice, although that was all that was meek about her. She often had opinions about others—how they dressed, how they spoke, how they behaved—that she was all too willing to share with them directly.

She also told me several times that she was uncomfortable singing the name "God" and flatly refused to sing "Jesus" or "Christ." Since we sang a fair bit of Christian sacred music, that became a problem for her, but I simply suggested she omit those words/notes when they occurred. She seemed OK with that solution.

During the last year of Sophie's life, her daughter called me to talk about how to keep her safe as she went to and from rehearsals. Sophie's mind had begun to fail, and in her late eighties, she died.

Sophie the soprano

Her daughter called me again then, but she didn't seem to remember my exact role with the Chorus: "You have no idea how much singing in the Chorus meant to my mother. She so looked forward to Tuesday evenings and hated to see the summer come because rehearsals would end for a few months." Then, in a moment of recognition, she asked, "So, are you the director of the Chorus? And did my mother bring you cookies?"

I said I was and that Sophie had brought me lots of things, especially baked goods. "Well then, you're the one she had a crush on!" she exclaimed.

I had no idea, but it did warm my heart to hear it, even after she was gone.

Sophie was such a timid singer she didn't really contribute much musically to the Chorus, but she didn't do any harm either. Bill would still scoop entrances from time to time, but I'd always give him a gentle, knowing look, and he'd usually smile and nod and try to get it right the next time.

I'm sure there's a CD out there somewhere with Bill scooping a pitch, and I'm sure there's a DVD showing Sophie refusing to sing "Jesus Christ." So, the recordings aren't perfect, and who cares? How much more important was it that their lives were enriched by the experience of singing in harmony with others? How much more important that the undergrad student who might one day be conducting a choir or leading some other group of people will be welcoming and supportive of an elderly person who needs a place to belong?

How much more important that every other member of the Chorus saw that inclusivity can enrich all our lives in countless ways.

Food for thought:

- How willing and able are you to tolerate imperfection?
- Does every member of your group feel welcome and valued, regardless of his or her level of ability and contribution?
- What more can you do to foster a spirit of inclusivity where you lead?

ⓗ Be Part of a Community

Most humans aren't happy being hermits. We are wired to be interactive, to live in community with others, to be interdependent. Despite the conflicts that communities inevitably endure, on balance, they provide the emotional sustenance we all need to be fulfilled and happy. The most effective communities are those where a common interest or purpose is shared. Musical groups are one of the best examples I know of a community with a shared purpose, and I feel privileged to have been the leader of many such groups.

My first opportunity to lead a choir was at First Christian Church in Carterville, Illinois, at the age of sixteen. I often advise young people interested in conducting to find a forgiving group, willing to overlook youthful foibles and mistakes. That's what I was fortunate to have in this choir—a group of adults mostly willing to try all the new things I was learning about good singing posture, breathing exercises, and the many other quirky things

First Christian Church, Carterville, Illinois

singers do. I was part of that community (being the preacher's kid didn't hurt), and they treated me with grace, allowing me to gain the experience and confidence I needed. Some of those singers are still close family friends to this day.

As mentioned earlier, I spent sixteen years at Northeastern Illinois University (NEIU) as Director of Choral Activities. The Music Department was struggling when I first arrived in the fall of 1996, and it was necessary to recruit residents from the surrounding area to join the University Chorus, simply to fill out the group and create better balance. As it turned out, including singers of all ages from outside the university created a much richer experience for all of us. In any given semester, fully half of the Chorus was comprised of non-students.

So, what would prompt twenty-five to thirty community residents to give up three hours every week to sing with a choir? I suppose one obvious reason is to experience the joy of making good music.

But I think it's not that simple. Solo singing is a wonderful experience, but it takes more voices to create harmony, and there's nothing quite like singing in harmony. To revel in the interplay of voices

Northeastern Illinois University Chorus

Inspiring Harmony

within an ensemble is to know what community is supposed to feel like. To ride the musical wave created by a community of musicians, sometimes supporting others, sometimes taking the lead, is to truly feel the rhythm of life.

One volunteer singer during my tenure at Northeastern, Robert Seid, who has since become a good friend, always seemed well attuned to the positive energy that accompanied his choral experience (and his life experience, I think). Once he got past the required audition to become a member of the Chamber Choir (an event that seemed to arouse great fear and trepidation), his joy in being part of the ensemble and making music was perpetually evident. I believe his association with the Choir enriched his life, and I'm sure he enriched the lives of those around him.

It's my good fortune that Bob is currently a video director at the Ravinia Festival in Chicago (my summer employment), so I continue to see and work with him regularly.

I submitted the text of this chapter to Bob for his approval before publishing, and I thought his response was worth repeating:

Robert Seid

> *… thank you for telling my story. Yes, I did get the positive physical, mental and emotional vibes from group singing, but just as important for me was the audition process and overcoming my fear and trepidation. I recall you would not accept a so-called Broadway show tune, like 'They Call the Wind Mariah' – not even 'Joey, Joey' from 'Most Happy Fella' would do.*
>
> *So, I got a book of old Italian songs. It came with a CD as a learning aid. I got a voice coach for two lessons and learned 'Vittoria, mio core,' including the bridge, and sang it to your accompaniment during the audition.*
>
> *Then you gave me a quiz about what key something was written in.*
>
> *I guessed 'E-flat,' and it turned out I was right.*
>
> *When you told me I was in, I jumped up and down with delight for a second. I recall your eyes bugging out a little at the spectacle.*

As a result of this newfound confidence, I successfully auditioned for [other choirs].

When you gave me a shot at choral singing after a three-decade layoff, it really did change my life in a positive way.

Then there are the extra-musical factors that serve to make the communal bond even stronger. At different times everyone will find joy, comfort, satisfaction, release, or just plain fun in making music with a group. Lifelong friendships are often born, romantic relationships develop, young and old sit and make music side by side, and people come together to work toward a common goal. I can't count the hours I've spent with choral friends and colleagues having a drink after a concert, a cup of coffee on a rehearsal break, or even playing racquetball for those of us with a competitive side.[1] Those experiences away from the rehearsal and concert halls serve to strengthen the bond a community of musicians feels when working together.

> [1] I began playing racquetball as an undergraduate student at the University of Iowa, and I have continued to play to this day. Although now, there seem to be more silver-haired players and the matches move a bit more slowly.

When I finished my sixteen years with the choirs at NEIU, they were kind enough to give a party in my honor. We all enjoyed some food and drink and shared stories about the concerts we had

Mike's NEIU farewell party with members of the Chorus and Chamber Choir

presented. But the most gratifying and moving part of the evening was to hear the testimonials given by several of the singers who had been with the choirs for more than a few years. One person after another spoke about how important the choirs had been in his or her life:

"My wife passed away, and singing in the Chorus provided me some much needed solace."

"I loved seeing the same people week after week and feeling like they were my family."

"It's so exciting when the orchestra comes and all the pieces fall into place to make one glorious sound."

"My week is so filled with work and other commitments, I like to have the pleasure of sitting in a choir rehearsal for a change of pace."

"Choir is my weekly respite, a chance to recharge my batteries."

The experience for most went beyond merely making music; it was more profound because the community grew and thrived.

To live alone is possible, but more like existing than truly living. To live and work and make music with others is to experience the joy, satisfaction, and fulfillment only a community can bring.

If music is not your calling, find something else that lights a fire in you, and do it with others. Open yourself up to the experience of being part of a group—to be vulnerable, to help someone else succeed, to work together toward a common goal. And if you are privileged to be the leader of a group, inspire others to find purpose in their mission, to find joy in working as a team, to be part of the community.

Food for thought:

- Are you part of a group that feels like your second family? Does the group you lead feel like a welcoming community for its members?

- Think of some activities that would promote a sense of connection, togetherness, and community in your organization.

Michael Melton

Make My Day

A large percentage of the students at Northeastern Illinois University (NEIU) are what we often term "non-traditional."

What does that mean exactly? Their lives don't follow the script many of us think of as "normal."

Of course that version of "normal" is based on the life experiences of those who have enjoyed more privilege or good fortune, which is really a minority of people. Many of my students there were the first in their families to attend a college or university. Many were paying their own way by holding down jobs while attending classes, which often extended their time to complete a degree by a year or more. Many had children and/or parents to care for. And many had received a poor high school education and were woefully in need of remedial tutoring and assistance just to be able to write a short essay.

The challenges, both academic and otherwise, were daunting for many.

One of my students, Maria (not her real name), had a mind-boggling array of family issues. Her brother had run-ins with the law and was shot and wounded by Chicago police when they claimed he was attempting to flee after being detained. Maria herself missed a class one day when she had to appear in court because she had kicked and injured another girl while trying to defend her pregnant sister from an imminent altercation.

I felt badly for Maria. Yes, she could have made some better choices, but she was a sweet young woman who deserved a chance to improve her lot in life. She told me about her situation on a few occasions, and I did my best to listen and offer her some support and encouragement.

In February 2013, after my father passed away,[1] I received a lovely card signed by many students

Inspiring Harmony

> [1] My parents were living in Tucson, Arizona, during my father's final illness, and I had to be away from the university to be with them, so students were aware of the situation.

and faculty from the NEIU Music Department.

Maria was the one who took it upon herself to gather signatures and present the card to me. It was a heartfelt gesture that I very much appreciated.

When I thanked her, she said, "You were there for me when I was going through some hard times, and I appreciated that, so I wanted to do this for you."

I remembered having listened to her when she was having trouble, but I really didn't think I had done anything special. It was obviously more meaningful and helpful to her than I realized, and I was especially honored sometime later when she told me I was the reason she decided to become a teacher.

Here is a lighter tale: My work as Score Reader for the Ravinia Festival is most often with the Chicago Symphony Orchestra. It's always fascinating for me to see how many experienced

Ravinia Festival stage with video screens and CSO

professionals in the orchestra care about whether their faces appear on the video screens where our IMAG (Image Magnification) production is projected. Some come to me privately to say they would rather not be on the screens. But many have come to say they have friends or family in the audience and would like to be on camera, especially during an important solo. The video director makes the call, of course, but I often will nudge him to find a moment to feature the orchestra member who asked for a close up. It's remarkable to see how much it means to them and how much they appreciate the attention—like a little solo bow, as it were.

I spent many years as a conductor trying every moment to raise the musical bar—nothing wrong with striving to be the best we can be—but I remember a university student after one rehearsal asking, "Aren't we doing anything right?"

It was another wake-up call for me to realize that a little compliment, a little encouragement, can go a long way. For musicians (and everyone else), I think it makes them want to be better and work harder, and in the end, that compliment produces better results. I don't advocate lavishing praise on a student who is not performing well, but finding something good to say about a person's performance will yield better long-term results, both personally and professionally, than brow-beating.

It really doesn't take much: a smile, a pat on the back, a compliment for a job well done, a listening ear, a caring card or email, or just sitting with someone for a few minutes, can all be the small, graceful gestures that make the difference in a person's day. As leaders, we often are so focused on the work at hand, we forget to compliment, nurture, and inspire our team. When we spare a moment for a little encouragement, we not only improve people's performance, we improve their lives.

Food for thought:

- Do you look for opportunities to offer a compliment or encouragement to your team?

- Are you sensitive to members of your group who may be a little down, slightly off their game, maybe even depressed?

- Do you encourage the members of your group to support one another—to hold each other up?

Inspiring Harmony

ⓗ Be a Teacher

How many books must there be espousing techniques and methods for being a good leader? Events abound—leadership conferences, workshops, seminars—everyone seems to have a different angle on becoming an effective leader, and businesses spend lots of money on leadership development. In my opinion, the most effective leaders are actually teachers. They don't dictate success; they engender it in others by teaching them how to succeed.

I've always been drawn to teaching, in part because my mother is a retired teacher. From the time I was a young child, I witnessed her devotion to teaching and her commitment to helping children learn to read. Her passion for education was much of my inspiration for becoming a teacher.

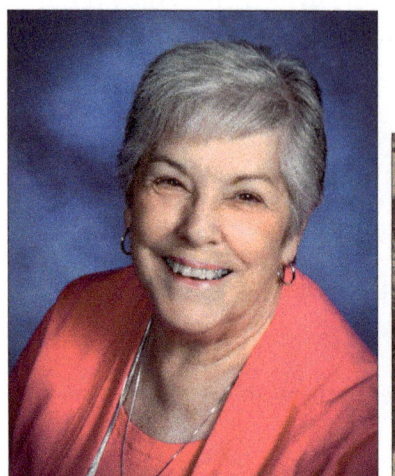

Teaching doesn't come naturally for everyone, but nearly anyone can adopt some of the most important characteristics of a good teacher. Other leadership books often focus on being a good communicator, but teaching goes a step further, ensuring that learning has actually occurred.

Mike's mother, Martha, and (right) with her second-grade students

Michael Melton

One of my favorite aviation writers, Rod Machado, wrote an excellent article a few years ago about this very subject, and I felt compelled to send him a congratulatory email.

When he wrote back to thank me, he said, "We all have to remember that telling is not teaching." (Mike Thompson, another aviation author and presenter, has published a book by the same name, *Telling Is Not Teaching*.) In fact, telling is not necessarily even communicating. Telling something to the group you are leading does not mean communication has taken place, let alone comprehension, agreement, or a plan for implementation.

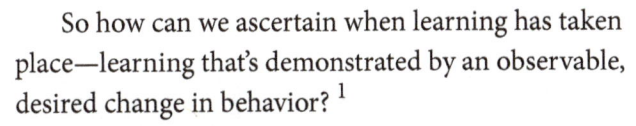

Rod Machado

So how can we ascertain when learning has taken place—learning that's demonstrated by an observable, desired change in behavior? [1]

> [1] Educational psychology and learning theories are ubiquitous, so distilling the concept of "learning" is a major challenge and, consequently, the subject of numerous books and dissertations.

Knowing with certainty can be a bit of a trick, thus the copious methods for assessment in contemporary education. While I agree that learning should be measured, it seems to me the tail is wagging the dog nowadays; more time is spent assessing than teaching, it seems. Finding a reliable tool for measuring learning is vitally important, but evaluation should not be an end in itself.

When I was supervising student teachers at Northeastern Illinois University (NEIU), I attended a meeting of supervisors where we were all handed a form to use for assessing our student teachers. I familiarized myself with the new form and used it for the next few weeks. At the next month's meeting we were handed another assessment form, which prompted me to remark that we had been given a new assessment form just the previous month.

The head of the Education Department chairing the meeting said—and I am *not* making this up—"This is the assessment form we're using to assess the new assessment form."

I laughed out loud, which caused her to bristle, but it was the

Mike's NEIU portrait

most ridiculous thing I'd ever heard.

The best teaching occurs when the teacher becomes the conduit rather than the focus of what is being taught. To be so self-important that the learning experience becomes more about the teacher than the subject is to completely miss the point.

In the case of art, it is the work itself that must be valued, studied, and ultimately understood. My college senior piano recital included Ravel's *Piano Concerto in G Major*, with my teacher, James Avery, playing the orchestral reduction. At the end of the recital, we came offstage together, and I turned to him and asked if he was pleased with my performance.

His answer was, "Don't do it for me—do it for Ravel."

An even more memorable example of proper focus was singing with the Grant Park Symphony Chorus with guest conductor Robert Shaw, who was described once by *The New York Times* as "the renowned choral conductor and the elder statesman and great spirit of American musical performance."

He came to Chicago to conduct the Mozart *Mass in c minor* ("Great") with the Grant Park Symphony Orchestra and Chorus. His rehearsals were inspiring—musically energetic, detailed without being tedious, and filled with new insights into this great masterpiece.

At the conclusion of our second and final room rehearsal (there are rarely more than two, often only one, with a

Robert Shaw

professional chorus and guest conductor), the Chorus offered heartfelt, extended applause for his good work.

After only a few moments, Shaw held up his conductor's score, as if to say, *Don't applaud me, applaud Mozart.*

He was truly the conduit through which we had gained valuable insight into a masterwork. He was a leader, but he was even more a teacher.

Unfortunately, I never had the chance to perform with Shaw conducting. That was the last concert of the season for the Grant Park Chorus, and we had failed to agree on a new contract that year. So the union voted to strike on the day of the concert, and the season ended without a performance of the "Great" *Mass in c minor*.

Not long after that (in 1999), Shaw passed away.

I've regretted missing out on performing with him, but I've always appreciated what he taught me about Mozart, about conducting, and about being a teacher and a servant of the music.

॰॰॰

Setting out to be a leader is a journey fraught with peril.

In fact, the most effective leaders are usually those who have grown into the role organically, rather than making it a goal unto itself.

Setting out to be a teacher, on the other hand, is a journey of love and devotion toward a higher purpose. It's more a calling than a job, requiring mastery of the subject at hand, the ability to teach it, the willingness to assess whether learning has taken place, and the passion to inspire others to act on what they have learned.

What I have learned over the years is, if you really want to understand something, try teaching it.

When you become a good teacher, leadership naturally follows.

Food for thought:

- Have you ever tried teaching? Choose an area in which you have passion, experience, and skill—then find or create an opportunity to teach others.

- If you are already teaching, good for you! Do you have valid and reliable methods for assessing whether your students are learning?

- Can you create opportunities for members of your team to teach something to the rest of the group? It's a fun and interesting way for everyone to learn.

ⓗ Suck It Up

Wouldn't it be just grand if life always went swimmingly? If our career choices always seemed to be the right ones? If every day felt satisfying, gratifying, and complete?

For most people, life isn't quite so rosy, so the next question has to be: "How will I respond to disappointment?"

The mantra in my career has been, "Always have a plan, then be willing to change it."

My plan has been questioned and changed so many times, the plan has often become difficult to decipher. It has always included music, teaching, and flying, not necessarily in that order, but the plan has suffered varying degrees of caprice, particularly when work on a job or project has soured. One thing I've learned over the years, however, is that chasing after the next exciting prospect when things get rough is ultimately futile. Following through on a commitment,

Michael Lorentz

regardless of the obstacles, is usually the more rewarding choice.

I've been score reading for video and televised productions of concerts since 1994, first with WTTW, a public television station in Chicago. The director with whom I've worked most, Michael Lorentz, has been a good friend and colleague, but one experience nearly ended our working relationship prematurely.

I've mentioned my work as a score reader previously, but I haven't fully explained what a score reader does. When a video projection or recording is to be made of a musical performance, the music is choreographed and the score(s) marked in advance based on several factors, including: the number of cameras and what each camera sees; the variation of the shots to show as much of the orchestra as possible; and most importantly, which instrument(s) or sections in the orchestra are most prominent at any given moment in the music. Of course, shots of the conductor are included, particularly from the orchestra's view—most audience members only get to see the conductor from behind, so it's interesting for them to see what the players see.

The scores are prepared and rehearsed by the video director and/or score reader. Then, at the performance/recording, the score reader follows the score, rhythmically counting the director into each shot as it comes. The director can then decide what to do with each shot to create the most artistic production.

For most recording projects, especially with many cameras, there are shot sheets for the camera operators so that everyone knows which camera shots are coming ahead of time.

For our work at the Ravinia Festival in Chicago, however, I prepare the scores in advance and feed information to the director on the fly (usually with only one rehearsal), which makes for some pretty intense and exciting performances.

In the late 1990s, WTTW hired me to score read for a live concert recording of the Chicago Symphony Orchestra, conducted by Daniel Barenboim. Since the video director, Mike, had already choreographed the scores as usual, my job was simply to put in the necessary counts ahead of each camera shot, follow along as the pieces were played, and count him into the shots.

The first sign of trouble came about three-quarters of the way through the concert when the executive producer came into the recording booth to tell me the maestro had asked for the score reader to note any problem spots that might need to be re-recorded.

"We're nearly finished with the concert, and I haven't been listening for that at all," I told her.

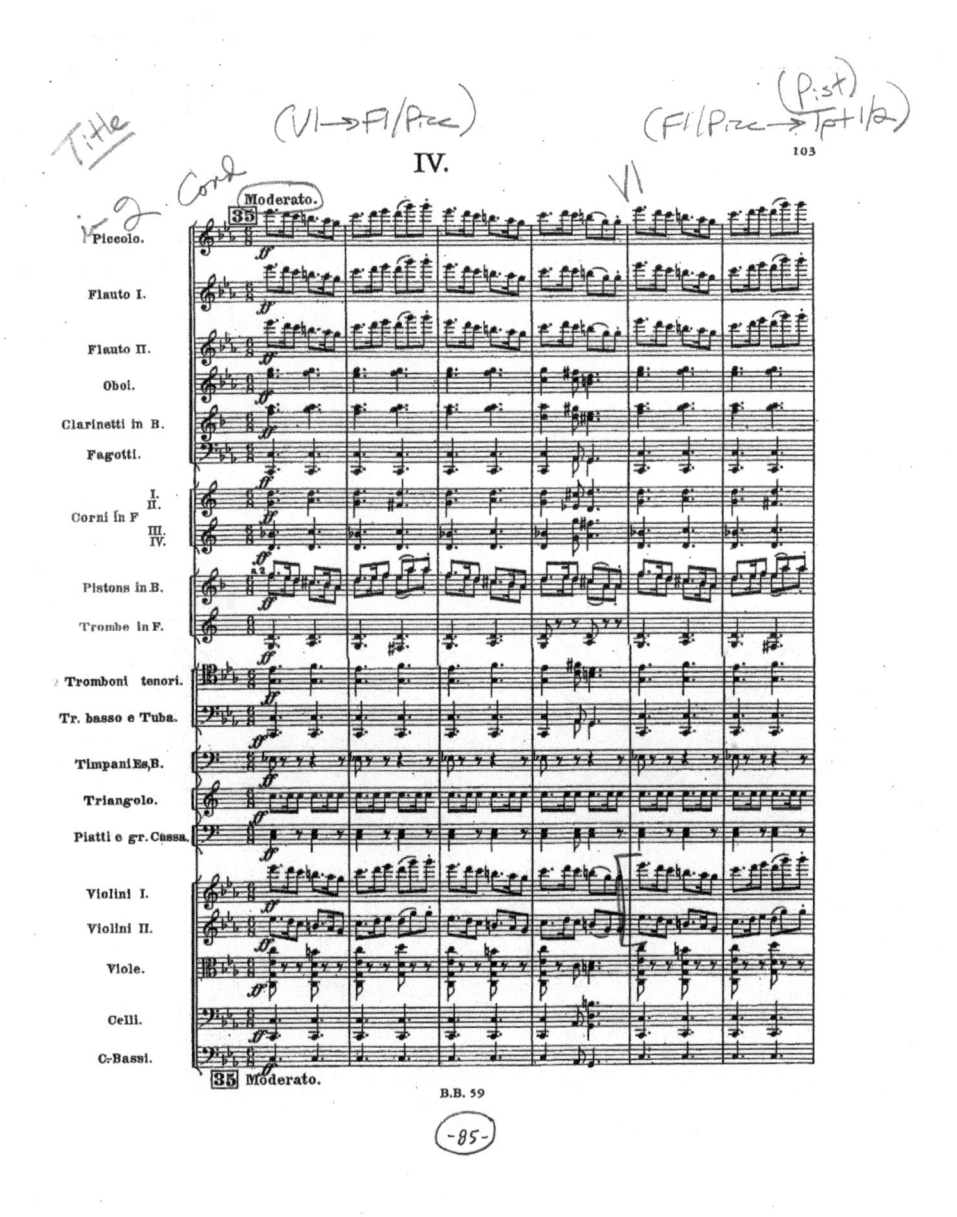

Page from a full score, prepared for video

She said, "Well, come up with something to tell him by the end of the concert."

When the concert ended, I quickly went back and found a spot I knew had been problematic; two minutes later she was back to say, "Let's go—the maestro is waiting."

Backstage, Barenboim was sweating and seemed very tense and uncomfortable.

I stood off to the side while he and others discussed what to do next.

Daniel Barenboim

Then the producer turned to me and asked, "Mike, do you have any suggestions for sections that might need to be re-recorded?"

"Well, there is one particular spot—" I offered.

"Yes, what is it!" Barenboim barked. (I'm afraid I don't respond very well to barking.)

So I knelt down next to the maestro, who was seated, and showed him my score. "From this section to the next," I said, pointing to the problem spot, "the marking is for *lo stesso tempo* (also, *l'istesso tempo,* meaning "the same tempo"), but your tempo in the new section was not the same, so there was some confusion."

"Well, how bad was it?" he snapped.

"Only a couple of beats for things to line up," I answered.

"Well then, forget it," he said.

I looked at the producer and said, "I think that's all I have."

After returning to the recording booth, I learned the orchestra would be replaying a section of a Ginastera[1] piece—one of the more difficult ones to read.

> [1] Alberto Ginastera was a 20th-century Argentine composer. Much of his music incorporates traditional Argentine folk themes and musical idioms.

I asked where Barenboim intended to start, but no one seemed to know. I kept insisting I needed to know a starting point, but Barenboim simply took off somewhere in the middle of the piece without warning and began to play the excerpt. I searched frantically to find my place in the score, but the excerpt was nearly finished by the time I found it. The video we got was completely useless.

The video director, Mike, was upset, and Barenboim was angry when he learned they would have to play it yet again. I felt embarrassed and responsible since my sole purpose there was to read the score, but not knowing where the orchestra was beginning made it a guessing game for me. Nevertheless, I took Mike's frustration personally and left that evening feeling like I had dropped the ball.

After thinking about it for a few days, I decided I'd had enough. The next time I got a call from WTTW to score read (if I ever did), I would say "no"—I wouldn't go through that again.

But, as time passed, I decided if they weren't happy with my work, they'd call someone else; if they wanted me back, they would say so.

So, when they did call again for another project, I said "yes."

It was several years later when the Ravinia Festival called Mike to ask if he would head up an IMAG (Image Magnification) project they had in mind for their annual Gala concert. He asked me to score read for that concert and for two more concerts the following summer. After that, Ravinia decided to start using IMAG for the entire summer season, and Mike said he wanted me to be there for all the concerts involving an orchestra. I was heartened by his faith in me and grateful he wanted me at Ravinia in that role.

After a few more years of working together, I asked Mike about that fateful night at Orchestra Hall with Barenboim and the CSO, and whether he knew how close I had come to giving up on score reading altogether. Surprisingly, he said he didn't even remember what had happened. Perhaps he was just being kind and allowing me to save face, I don't know. But, had I said "no" years earlier after the fiasco, I would have missed out on many years of fulfilling, enjoyable work at Ravinia.

Working and personal relationships, especially when leading groups, can sometimes be frustrating, maddening, embarrassing, disappointing, and seemingly hopeless. Finding grace in those moments can truly be a challenge. And there are indeed times when it's best to walk away. But more often, it pays to stick with it, lose the defensiveness, take a deep breath, and suck it up.

Food for thought:

- Can you remember a time when you were ready to throw in the towel? Do you have coping mechanisms to help put it all into perspective? To take a step back from the edge and know that "this, too, shall pass?"

- Do you have a close friend and confidant to rely on when things seem hopeless? Cultivate a friendship like that with care.

Michael Melton

♪ You Never Arrive

What does it mean to "go out on top"? On top compared to what? Your peers? Some arbitrary standard? Someone's notion of perfection or at least completion?

To feel a sense of satisfaction and gratification for our accomplishments is understandable, but to believe we've arrived, with nothing more to learn or achieve, is shortsighted and naïve.

Let's recap …

Most of my youth was spent in Carterville, Illinois, a town of about 3,000 people at the time—my high school graduating class was ninety-three. I had some musical talent, and performing around town was how I got my strokes, so becoming a teenaged, go-to musician was a fairly easy role to fall into. I played piano, sang, and led the choir at church, played piano and organ and sang for countless weddings and funerals, and blew taps on my cornet for Veteran's Day memorial events.

It felt good being one of the best musicians in town, especially at such a young age.

After high school, I decided to attend Southern Illinois University (SIU) in Carbondale. My high school music teacher

Mike in his marching band uniform – 7th grade

was encouraging me to go to a more challenging school, but SIU was close by, I had already been studying piano with a professor there, and I graduated from high school at seventeen, so I made a safe choice by attending SIU. I found a little more competition there than I experienced in Carterville, but I soon found my niche and took my place among the better students.

At the end of my sophomore year at SIU, my parents moved to Iowa City, Iowa. I decided to move with them and transfer to the University of Iowa. In hindsight, it became clear I should have moved away from home at that point for my own personal development, but the move to the university was a good one.

Again the competition was stiffer than before. I did manage to find my place and succeed, but it was becoming increasingly obvious that most of the other students I met had also been among the best musicians in their own hometowns. I was beginning to understand what it felt like to be a small fish in a big pond.

Later, in 1982, after two years of junior high school teaching and a master's degree from Iowa, I moved to Chicago to become Music Director of the Chicago Children's Choir. I also began singing with the Chicago Symphony Chorus that year.

As I became acquainted with other professional musicians in Chicago, the "small fish/big pond" metaphor took on a whole new meaning. I knew I could compete, but having things fall into my lap because everyone just knew I was good simply didn't happen. I was constantly reminded of how I needed to continue to improve if I wanted to sustain my career. Fortunately, I could both sing and play piano in a variety of styles, conduct, and teach; otherwise, I might not have been able to piece together even a modest living.

I've been reminded again and again that the more I know, the more I have to learn. Performing with and observing the greatest musicians in the world with the Chicago Symphony, Grant Park Symphony, and Lyric Opera of Chicago was both exhilarating and humbling. I could look back at my youthful experiences and realize how far I had come, then watch masterful conductors, such as Erich Leinsdorf, Zubin Mehta, James Levine, and Sir Georg Solti—and know how much more I had to learn.

When my students come to me to say how impressed they are with my abilities, I tell them the story of Claudio Abbado, the great conductor who died in 2014.

In 1984, I sang with a small ensemble from the Chicago Symphony Chorus in a partially staged production of Alban Berg's *Wozzeck*, conducted by Abbado. *Wozzeck* is a challenging 20th-

Michael Melton

Claudio Abbado

century opera: In avant-garde style, it utilizes atonality and *Sprechgesang* ("speech song"—an expressionist vocal technique between speaking and singing, with approximate pitch).

As was often the case, Abbado led rehearsals with only a pocket score[1] for reference, and he conducted the performances entirely from memory. (I'm told that was due, in part, to his poor eyesight.) Nonetheless, it was always impressive to see how well he knew the score. I was astounded after the first performance when I stopped in to say hello to the librarian, Marilyn.

She said Abbado had come by immediately after the concert to give her twenty-nine corrections that he wanted put into some of the players' parts. He had not only conducted the entire work from memory, but had catalogued in his mind twenty-nine mistakes that needed correction before the next evening's performance. And these weren't general comments like "Play Act 2 louder"—they were specific comments like "The second bassoon played a d-sharp in measure 429, and it should be a d-natural."

It was an incredible feat, and one I still remember when I feel like resting on my laurels. I use this story to teach my students that, no matter how far we've come, there is always someone out there to set the bar higher.

[1] *Also known as a "miniature score," pocket scores are used primarily for score study. They can be difficult for a conductor to use in rehearsal or performance simply because they are so small—all the more reason a conductor would have to know a piece very well to do it.*

∽∽∽

As leaders, we have a responsibility to spur ourselves and encourage those we lead to continually stretch, grow, and flourish. The way to live a vibrant, fulfilling life to the end is to continue to learn.

Gaining knowledge and insight requires work, but satisfaction comes with exploration and delight with discoveries made along the way.

Be inspired by the artistry and creativity of others. Fall in love with the very act of learning. And remember that life itself is a journey—you never actually arrive.

Food for thought:

- Do you still find joy in learning?

- If you've been leading or teaching for a long time (especially the same subjects in the same place), how long has it been since you researched new methods and materials?

- When was the last time you attended a conference or seminar for some fresh inspiration? What ideas did you incorporate into your own work?

Michael Melton

♭ Bloom Where You're Planted

Like so many other young people with a passion and a dream, I was ready to take the musical world by storm from the time I was in my late teens. I had, after all, been the star of the show at so many church and school events within a sixty-mile radius of my hometown, how could the musical world possibly not recognize that I was here to change it for the better? It seemed perfectly obvious to me.

After arriving in Chicago in 1982 and joining the Chicago Symphony Chorus, it was also clear to me that I should one day be conducting the Chicago Symphony Orchestra. I even carried a baton, just in case the conductor took ill and they needed me to step in. I always told myself there wasn't a snowball's chance of that ever happening, but I carried it anyway, just because you never know …

I've since come to learn that you must be careful what you wish for. More than once I've seen a conductor be chewed up and spit out by some orchestra members, simply because they

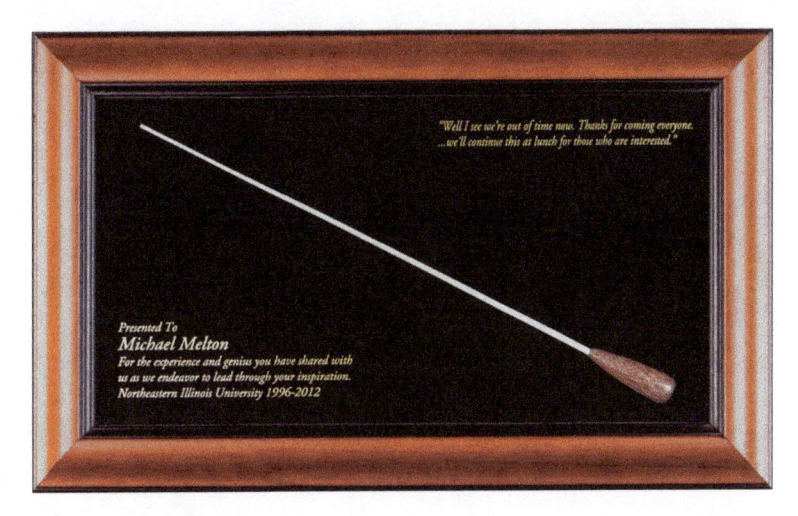

Mike's conducting baton, presented by NEIU students

Inspiring Harmony

judged the conductor to be less than fully qualified. It can be a tricky business, and I doubt I would have fared much better.

Well, the Chicago Symphony Orchestra didn't come knocking at my door, and I instead conducted church, school, and community choirs. Those experiences were generally worthwhile, but I often felt as though my talents and skills were being under-utilized.

As I've mentioned, when I joined the faculty at Northeastern Illinois University (NEIU) in 1996, the Music Department was in a rebuilding stage. I felt frustrated, and after a few years I was ready to walk away. In fact, I had packed up my personal things to take home one day when I ran into Nelson, the department chair, on my way out of the building.

When he asked what I was up to, I told him I had had enough and would talk to him about it later. He called me later and kindly helped talk me off the ledge, for which I will be forever grateful.

But I had equally important conversations with others in the department. My studio partner and fellow voice teacher, Ron Combs, listened to me complain one day about the unrefined performances of some of our students. His wise counsel to me was, "Remember Mike, no matter how far we've come or how much experience we have, when the freshmen arrive here, most of them are only eighteen—every year."

Ronald Combs

I also remember talking with our staff accompanist, Jane Kenas-Heller, whom I had known when I was conducting and she was accompanying the Park Ridge (Illinois) Chorale. (Park Ridge is Hillary Clinton's hometown.) Jane helped me better understand our mission at NEIU and the value of the work we were all doing there. We talked about how the makeup of the Music Department was anything but "white bread." Our students came from so many different, often challenging situations, and simply didn't fit any particular mold.

Jane Kenas-Heller

"Most importantly," she said, "you can teach and inspire and help these students." It may have been the first time I really began to get my head out of the clouds and see my career and myself in a more realistic way.

What I eventually came to learn was that I was being helped and inspired more than the students. I was honing my own skills as a teacher and conductor, but at the same time, I was finding ways to be a positive influence on students' lives. Like every other faculty member, I was interested in helping students prepare for careers as performers or teachers, but I found myself in the position of influencing their lives in ways far more important than their study of music.

Mike with NEIU students

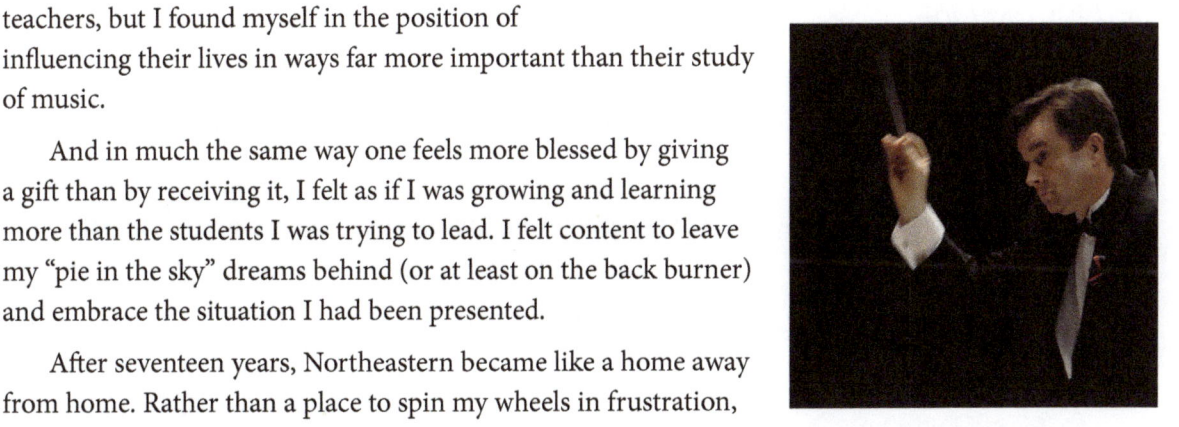

And in much the same way one feels more blessed by giving a gift than by receiving it, I felt as if I was growing and learning more than the students I was trying to lead. I felt content to leave my "pie in the sky" dreams behind (or at least on the back burner) and embrace the situation I had been presented.

After seventeen years, Northeastern became like a home away from home. Rather than a place to spin my wheels in frustration, it proved to be a place to mature, a place to nurture and be nurtured, a place to teach and make music, and a place to help guide some young students as they struggled to find their paths in life. It became a place to feel fulfilled in my work and to believe I had made a difference in peoples' lives.

Mike conducting the Mozart Requiem *at NEIU*

It wasn't the Chicago Symphony Orchestra, but as time went on, that really didn't matter.

> [1] Aside from his inspired work as a conductor, Robert Shaw was also a gifted writer.
> In letters to his singers, beginning with the salutation "Dear people," he shared his philosophies and musical insights in profound and colorful ways.

The great conductor Robert Shaw said, "I've learned that you grow the best vegetables in your own back yard." [1]

The best-laid plans, youthful visions, and lofty goals may not always come to fruition, but I've come to learn—and this is important—blooming where you're planted is not the same as settling. Good leaders can have a meaningful, positive impact on the lives of others, wherever they may find themselves. Ambition can be a double-edged sword: a good motivator and a blinding obsession at the same time. If you end up at the top of your field, whatever that may mean, good for you. But for the other 99 percent of us, life will be happier and more gratifying if we learn to bloom where we're planted.

Food for thought:

- Have you aspired to great things, but feel you've missed the mark? Still waiting to be discovered? In the meantime, are you making the most of the situation in which you find yourself right now?

- Take a good look at the members of the group you lead. Are you having a positive impact on their lives? And they on yours?

- Is life passing you by while you wait for "something better" to come along?

ⓗ Live in Grace

If anyone were to ask me how to fix the world (surprisingly, no one has), these are the three words I would say: Live in grace.

I feel inadequate to fully explain grace, but I'm hopeful every effort to do so may bring us all a little closer to understanding and living it. For leaders, grace should permeate everything we do.

As a child, I learned about God's unconditional love as an expression of God's grace. I remember how comforting it was to know I was saved by God's grace, especially because I really did not want to go to Hell, and I really did seek my parents' approval. (Although, at the time, my parents' disapproval scared me more than Hell.)

My whole concept of God and God's grace has changed significantly since then, but I still think of it as a wonderful way to find spiritual wholeness and joy.

Over the years, grace has taken on a much broader meaning for me. I believe if the thoughts and actions of every individual were to be imbued with grace (a tall order, to be sure), there would simply be no conflict. To live in grace means to put the needs and best interests of others before your own, to treat others as you would want to be treated, to be willing to bend to the needs, desires, and demands of others, to be both graceful and gracious.

In a world driven mostly by greed and fear, putting others first may seem a daunting task and a recipe for losing, but it's the only way for the community to truly thrive.

Getting everyone on board with the idea is the perpetual challenge.

So, what happens when someone else decides not to get on board and manages to hurt you, whether inadvertently or willfully?

The common admonition is to forgive—a skill that must be carefully cultivated and is rarely perfected. But does turning the other cheek mean allowing oneself to be run over because of another's careless or pernicious actions? How many times must we forgive? Don't we have the right to defend ourselves? Isn't life supposed to be fair?

These are difficult questions without clear answers. One thing I do know: To carry the hurt from an offense can become a heavy burden, but forgiveness can lighten the load.

I find this the most important, but most difficult lesson for leaders to learn. People in groups seem to feel less personal responsibility and accountability than do individuals, and they often permit themselves to criticize more harshly from within a group (or anonymously) than they would one on one. Such attacks can leave us feeling defeated and disinclined to exhibit grace. But that is precisely when living in grace becomes even more imperative.

Sometimes grace is displayed in the smallest of ways. My first time in a Catholic church was at age eighteen and at the invitation of a priest who invited me to sing for a Mass.

Having spent my entire (short) life in evangelical churches, attending Mass was a new and mysterious experience for me. I paid close attention to everything that transpired, and at a certain point, the priest said "Peace be with you." And the congregation responded, "And also with you."

Then he said, "Share with one another the sign of peace."

I assumed this was the point where you shook hands with a few people and asked if they got the crops in.

Instead, an older gentleman with a kind face came all the way across the sanctuary to where I was seated alone, shook my hand, and said, "The peace of Christ be with you."

I was taken aback at what appeared to be an extraordinarily generous gesture, this man coming all the way across the church to say such a lofty and lovely thing to me.

So I looked him in the eye and responded, "Well, thanks a lot."[1]

---

[1] *The usual appropriate responses are "And also with you;" "Peace be with you;" "The peace of Christ;" or simply, "Peace."*

He looked at me oddly for a moment, then squeezed my hand with both of his, smiling with what I later realized was a knowing smile.

It was a small gesture perhaps, but it made me feel comfortable, welcome, and appreciated—it was a gracious thing to do.

Living in grace is life's paramount challenge. I suppose if we all could fully achieve grace, we would have discovered nirvana, or Heaven on Earth. We would have learned to love one another unconditionally. I imagine we'd all spend a lot of time bowing to each other.

Like many ideals, it may seem unattainable, but I think there is virtue and ennoblement in trying.

❧ ❧ ❧

The most important lesson put simply: Grace is the answer.

No matter the conflict, no matter the challenge, no matter the disappointment, no matter the hurt … Grace is the answer.

Everyone should strive to live in grace, but leaders are held to a higher standard – we are particularly compelled to consistently show grace by our words, our actions, and our example. Be ever mindful of your calling.

You can truly change your little corner of the world by leading with grace.

Food for thought:

- What does living in grace mean to you?
- Who is the leader that most exhibits grace to you and why?

As I was making the final preparations to publish this book, President George H.W. Bush passed away. His pastor, The Rev. Russell J. Levenson, Jr., gave the homily at the funeral mass at the National Cathedral. He referenced a plaque given to him by the President, which included a quote, often misattributed to St. Francis of Assisi: "Preach the gospel at all times, and, if necessary, use words."

I would take the liberty of amending the admonition as a suitable conclusion to my thoughts: "Always exhibit grace, and, if necessary, use words."

Music has always provided the opportunity for me to lead. What opportunities are there for you?

The lessons I've learned and shared in this book have taken me part way toward living in grace. I believe they have made me a more compassionate and effective leader. I hope they will help you in your quest to find grace and to inspire harmony in those you lead.

Good luck on your journey ... *Buen Camino.*

Acknowledgments

Put me onstage to perform music, and I feel right at home. But this, my first attempt at writing a book, felt as if I were redefining "fish out of water" with every new page. I embraced the challenge because I had stories to tell, and I very much wanted to share my ideas about leading with grace. While the myriad steps from the germ of an idea to a finished book were sometimes daunting, I'm forever grateful for the assistance and guidance I received along the way.

I'm thankful to my friend and colleague, Bruce Lorie, for his painstaking efforts to organize, prepare, and produce the images for this project. His work has made the book visually rich, and I believe the images serve to enhance and draw the reader into the story.

I'm thankful to my mother, Martha, for her editorial suggestions and for checking my stories for accuracy. We've agreed the stories told here are at least mostly accurate.

I'm thankful to my wife, Arlis, for giving me the idea to write this book in the first place, and for her help fleshing it out. She has been a very successful leader in her own career as a human resources executive, and her expertise and creative ideas were enormously helpful to me.

I'm thankful to my eagle-eyed proofreader, Dave Peterson, for bringing fresh eyes to this project. His resolute attention to detail has made this a more accurate and handsome book.

I'm especially thankful to my editor and designer, Wynne Brown, without whose guidance I could not have successfully completed this book. Her patient and stalwart counsel as I took each next step provided me the sure footing I needed to navigate the murky waters of publishing a book. She went well beyond editing to teach me about virtually every aspect of the publishing process, and did so with grace.

Photo Credits and Sources

Images are privately owned by the author or in the public domain unless indicated below:

Page

8	Robert Kingsbury	Courtesy of Find-A-Grave
9	Howard Brown	Courtesy of the Newberry Library
11	Southern Illinois Christian Service Camp	Courtesy of Kaleb Smith
13	Daisy Duke	Photo from Wikimedia Foundation
16	Country church	Photo by Lonnie Webster, photographer
25	Don V Moses	Courtesy of Don V Moses
26	Sir Georg Solti	Lebrecht Music & Arts / Alamy Stock Photo
27	Fiora Contino	Photo by Frederic Contino, Creative Commons
42	Christopher Moore	1980 Press Photo of Christopher Moore, via the Historic Images Outlet
42	Martha Swisher	Courtesy of Martha Swisher

Michael Melton

43	Keith Hampton	Courtesy of Keith Hampton
46	Chicago Children's Choir	By arrangement with Johnson Publishing Co, Chicago
50	Margaret Hillis	Photo by Jim Steere, courtesy of Rosenthal Archives, Chicago Symphony Orchestra
55	John Jacob Niles	From www.johnjacobniles.com
56	Cynthia Yeh	Courtesy of Todd Rosenberg Photography, Cyntha Yeh, and the Chicago Symphony Orchestra
59	Sir Georg Solti	Courtesy of BBC Photo Library
66	Dennis Burmeister	Courtesy of Dennis Burmeister
70	Petrillo Music Shell, Chicago	Photo by Torsodog, Creative Commons
70	Thomas Peck	1994 Press Photo from the Historic Images Outlet
73	Rabbi Irving Glickman	Courtesy of Ronna Sharp
80	Navigation instruments	Courtesy of Jeremy Hampton, Final Approach Photography
89	Leonard Bernstein	Photo by Jack Mitchell
92	James Lucas	Courtesy of James Lucas
101	Garrison Keillor	Photo by Andrew Harrer / Bloomberg News / Landov
108	Robert Seid	Courtesy of Robert Seid
112	Ravinia Stage	Patrick Gipson/Ravinia Festival/2013
115	Rod Machado	Courtesy of Rod Machado

116	Robert Shaw	Courtesy of Special Collections and Archives, Georgia State University Library
122	Daniel Barenboim	Gobierno de la Ciudad Autónoma de Buenos Aires, Creative Commons
127	Claudio Abbado	From medicitv.com
130	Ronald Combs	Courtesy of Ronald Combs
130	Jane Kenas-Heller	Courtesy of Jane Kenas-Heller

Michael Melton

CPSIA information can be obtained
at www.ICGtesting.com
Printed in the USA
BVHW062110120320
574849BV00002B/25